THE
COFF

D1334011

"Kieron O'Hara and Nigel Shadbolt have offered an engaging and thought-provoking roadmap for the emerging field of Web Science. They crisply survey what lies ahead as the Web becomes ubiquitous, and they invite everyone – not just academics and experts – to think about how to preserve the Web's magic while avoiding its most unsettling prospects."

Jonathan Zittrain, Professor of Internet Governance and
Regulation, Oxford University

"Worried about the potential effect of new digital technologies on your personal privacy? Providing the most up-to-date information on this fascinating debate, the authors explore how technology has been infiltrating and changing our society."

Fred Piper, Director of the Royal Holloway Information Security Group,
University of London

"... an insightful commentary on what technology can do and on what individuals can do to protect themselves from unwanted intrusions made possible by new digital technologies."

Robin Mansell, Head of the Department for Media and Communications,
London School of Economics and Political Science

"*The Spy in the Coffee Machine* is an invaluable work for those of use who care about privacy but are baffled by technology."

Gareth Crossman, Director of Policy at the human rights organization Liberty

"This forward-looking book will introduce you to concepts like the Semantic Web, AJAX, Web 2.0, and pervasive computing – all terms you need to know about to protect yourself online – AND to get the most out of the Internet. The Web we know today is only the beginning!"

Robert Ellis Smith, Publisher of the Privacy Journal *newsletter since 1974*

ABOUT THE AUTHORS

Kieron O'Hara is Senior Research Fellow in Electronics and Computer Science at the University of Southampton, UK. He is the author or co-author of nine other books about technology, politics and society, including *Inequality.com: Power, Poverty, and the Digital Divide*, also published by Oneworld.

Nigel Shadbolt is Professor of Artificial Intelligence at the University of Southampton, UK, and was President of the British Computer Society in its 50th anniversary year 2006–2007. He is Chief Technology Officer of Internet security firm Garlik, and a director of the Web Science Research Initiative. He is both a chartered psychologist and a chartered engineer, and sits on a number of UK national science and technology committees.

THE SPY IN THE COFFEE MACHINE

KIERON O'HARA AND NIGEL SHADBOLT

ONEWORLD

OXFORD

A Oneworld Book

Published by Oneworld Publications 2008
Copyright © Kieron O'Hara and Nigel Shadbolt, 2008

ISBN: 978–1–85168–554–7

Typeset by Jayvee, Trivandrum, India
Cover design by Keenan Design
Printed and bound in the United States of America

Oneworld Publications
185 Banbury Road
Oxford OX2 7AR
England
www.oneworld-publications.com

Learn more about Oneworld. Join our mailing list to
find out about our latest titles and special offers at:

www.oneworld-publications.com

CONTENTS

PREFACE

The relationship between society and technology is complex, particularly as each has unpredictable effects on the other. We, as technologists, can talk until we are blue in the face about what is *possible*, or will be possible in the next few years. That's our favourite subject. But what will people want to use? What technologies will 'fit into' particular social niches? What technologies will remould society in their own images? These are tricky questions, and the correct answers can make you very rich. Wrong guesses, in a dynamic industry, can kill a firm or a reputation stone dead. Potential is huge, but not all nifty gizmos can define the future.

The need to understand these looping influences between society and technology has led to the evolution of a new discipline: Web Science. The Web is, in effect, a series of protocols defining how different computers talk to each other, but those protocols have massive real-world effects, which in turn create demands for new protocols and technologies. The aim of the recently-created Web Science Research Initiative, a joint venture between the University of Southampton and the Massachusetts Institute of Technology, is to hone the intellectual tools to study these developmental cycles. This book is part of the Web Science programme.

There are two things that technologists *can* be reasonably confident about. First, given enough history (and the electronic computer now does have a decent history behind it – one of us has recently been privileged to serve as the President of the British Computer Society in its 50th year), we can identify general trends. And second, understanding what is possible will tell us what social norms and attitudes are under threat. If a technology is sufficiently widespread, and becoming more so, then it may be that a particular set of cultural or political assumptions is no longer tenable.

It is our contention that privacy, since the Enlightenment a key pillar of the liberal ideal, is one of these somewhat obsolete norms in the face of the rapid spread of information technology. Information about one can be stored, found and passed around with almost trivial ease, and it is getting increasingly hard for the subject to retain control.

This means a political rethink, for sure. But it is not our contention that we are about to descend into a *Nineteen Eighty-Four*-style nightmare. It is cultural determinism of the worst sort to assume that society, politics and philosophy cannot adapt to the technology, and outright pessimism to suggest that the technology cannot be brought to heel by a sufficiently vigilant, engaged and educated society.

What is true is that the twentieth-century ideal of the private space will need to evolve, and that, if we truly value our privacy, we will have to play a much more active role in keeping it in place. The technologies that threaten can also be used to protect, and awareness is an important factor in their advantageous deployment. Education is vital; so is a public spirit (some of the gains from privacy accrue more to the community as a whole than to the individual, and therefore sometimes preserving privacy is a matter of altruism or social responsibility). Fatuous claims of the 'if you have nothing to hide you have nothing to fear' sort need to be resisted just as much as the puerile conspiracy theories that plague our political discourse.

We need debate, but for that debate to be worth having we need a much greater level of awareness of the technology to be diffused throughout society. This book is a small contribution to that task.

The field which we have surveyed is a wide one, and of course we have incurred many intellectual debts in our researches. A full list of acknowledgements would be prohibitively large, but in particular we would like to thank Wendy Hall, Brian Collins, Tim Berners-Lee, Tom Ilube, Pete Bramhall, Fred Piper and Kenny Paterson, members of the EPSRC Memories for Life network, the Office of Science and Technology's Foresight Programme on Cyber Trust and Crime Prevention, the Information Assurance Advisory Council, and the Defence Science and Technology Laboratory, and audiences at the 19th Hewlett-Packard Symposium on Information Security, the Royal Military College of Science, Shrivenham and the Bournemouth Media School. Many thanks also to Susan Davies (as ever), and Marsha Filion of Oneworld.

At the risk of allowing our private lives to encroach on the public space, KOH is deeply grateful to Rebecca Hughes for letting him fill the house with books, and NRS would like to thank Beverly Saunders for simply being there.

1

THE CASE OF THE DISAPPEARING BODY

… he that increaseth knowledge increaseth sorrow.

Ecclesiastes 1.18

THE BODY DISAPPEARS

In the words of the poem, 'Yesterday upon the stair, I met a man who wasn't there.' This was meant to be humorous: we can presume its author (one Hughes Mearns, since you ask) wasn't expecting it to be prescient. Nonetheless, it was.

A century after the lines were composed, we live in a society where *all the time* we meet men and women who aren't there. Acquaintance used to be face-to-face, a firm handshake, getting the cut of someone's jib. Trust was a matter of direct, personal acquaintance.[1] But the needs of a complex society, and a set of new technologies, changed all that.

The proportion of significant face-to-face contacts is falling all the time, in what has been called by sociologists the 'disappearance of the body'. We communicate by phone, email, letter, text; increasingly many of the contacts that make up our society are mediated through technology. Technological representations of ourselves do the interacting.

Mearns' poem has a very intriguing third line: 'He wasn't there again today.' The man who wasn't there makes a reappearance. But how can the narrator of the poem know that the man who wasn't there today was *the same* man who wasn't there yesterday? A nonsensical question? Hardly. If the man in the poem *was* there yesterday and today, it would be a trivial matter of memory to check whether he was the same on each day. Of course, the narrator can be fooled, by identical twins or a master of disguise. But the procedure is simple – recognising the same face, voice and mannerisms. Our brains have evolved over millions of years to do precisely that. And our society has augmented these methods with others to deal with less familiar persons – signatures, seals and passwords.

But a man who *isn't* there? None of these standard high-bandwidth methods will work for the absent presence. Instead, our mysterious bodiless fellow must work through some technologically-constructed version of himself or 'avatar'. Some trace must be left behind which leaves a trail back to the person whose body has disappeared, and those traces can be compared. Having met a man on the stair who wasn't there twice running, we might ask him a question about his mother's maiden name, or demand a digital signature, or get him to key in a digital password or PIN number.

PLENTY OF EVIDENCE

This leads to a strange paradox. A physical presence leaves behind few signs; a handshake in a closed room leaves no trace, except in the memory. Information, on the other hand, persists. In the case of the physical meeting, if something can be converted into information – via a bug, CCTV, or even DNA – then it could be established that the meeting really took place. Nevertheless, that is always an *extra* procedure, which could in principle be dodged by the people involved. But the man who isn't there must present some tangible piece of information to assure everyone else about his identity, which will remain as a semi-permanent testimony. With the disappearing body, the trace is intrinsic to the meeting taking place at all. No information, no meeting.

Each time a new technology appears that allows people to communicate without an immediate physical presence, a new abstraction is created. It may be an email log, a digital representation of non-verbal communication, a certificate of trustworthiness or whatever. But the abstraction has a concrete form in which the interaction lives on. As our bodies disappear, we leave more of these representations behind. It becomes harder to conceal what we have been doing. The technology boosts our privacy in the present (we don't have to meet people face to face), but it threatens the privacy of our past.

A number of technologies have affected the value, function and feasibility of privacy directly. In a wholly oral culture, spying requires someone to be within earshot of a conversation while simultaneously being concealed. Certain types of behaviour can only be performed in private if there are appropriate spaces protecting privacy. Even very simple technologies such as writing, walls and glass windows have effects on the private space; some give privacy, while others take it away.

The serious academic and legal interest in privacy[2] really began with the development of portable photographic cameras. With their invention, one could be wandering down the street, in public, but find one's image captured, and possibly printed using new printing techniques in journals. Although nothing in the situation took place in private before the technology appeared, there was a powerful intuition that one's privacy had somehow shrunk. In the nineteenth century, this was new and serious; nowadays, it is an issue only for those unfortunate enough to be of interest to tabloid newspapers. We are all used to our images being plundered, either by photographers or CCTV cameras, and we probably act accordingly. We are perhaps somewhat less likely to spit, pick our noses or urinate in the street, for instance, if we believe that we might be seen doing so (although a quick search through video-posting site YouTube will show many instances of unusual or noteworthy behaviour captured and preserved forever). And the whole point of a CCTV camera is to make us less likely to commit assaults or thefts, crimes which (if we are to avoid capture) have to be performed to some extent in privacy.

In this book, we want to explore the effects of new digital technologies on our privacy. There is no doubt that those technologies have the potential to be very injurious. It is hard to generalise – in individual cases the gains and losses, costs and benefits have to be weighed in the balance, and we shouldn't prejudge. Sometimes society benefits more than the individual loses. Sometimes the individual gains enough to justify the sacrifice of privacy. Sometimes the loss of privacy translates into a loss for society and a gain only for the state or the corporation. Very rarely is the effect catastrophic. And the costs and benefits vary; all governments misuse some data, and all governments use other data wisely, but one would be sensible to take different precautions depending on where one was. The demands of, say, the United States, France, Iran, China, Russia and North Korea are not the same, and each government has different aims, different ideologies, different dogmas and different scruples in dealing with its citizens.

Costs and benefits are the nub of the classic type of privacy problem – there are many tangible benefits to be gained by allowing intrusions into one's life, but there is also the intangible worry. We simply find it hard, as humans, to balance the tangible benefits and the intangible costs. In an evil dictatorship, one has a good idea of how personal information will be used, and so can plan accordingly. But in a capitalist democracy, it is much harder to decide how information will be used in the future. The benefits are there for all to see; the costs are not. This may be why our defences are so often down when our privacy is threatened.

Legislation is rarely the answer to our online problems. The law is intended to constrain technologists, but equally the technological capabilities constrain what the lawyers and the legislators can achieve. This rapidly evolving and unstable situation affects our understanding of privacy itself.

Applying apparently well-understood political principles is surprisingly hard in cyberspace, where we often find ourselves having to approve or disapprove of an outcome we never anticipated, or alternatively find ourselves having to decide about a principle that never seemed controversial or even relevant before.[3] Where do our rights to free speech end? Do you have an inalienable right to deliver an online lecture in the US to an audience in China? Do the disadvantages incurred by those who lack computer literacy or training fatally undermine their rights to just treatment by society? How far is a society justified in promoting computer literacy? To what extent is it reasonable for a technophobic refusenik to opt out of an information society? Is there a difference in kind between unauthorised exposure of, say, a photograph by hand to a few dozen people, and uploading a digital image to a website that receives thousands of visits a day?

Important questions of principle appear suddenly from nowhere as a result of technological development, and one either has to reinterpret old principles radically in the new space, or start to think anew. Google is responsible for about half the Web searches made worldwide; finishing low down in Google's page rankings can dramatically reduce visits to a site. What responsibilities does Google have for ensuring equitable treatment? Google's PageRank algorithm works by analysing the eigenvectors of the Web's link matrix – are any principles of fair and equitable treatment somehow breached in the design of the algorithm? Did any moral philosopher ever wonder about the rights and wrongs of eigenvector analysis (our guess: an emphatic no)? What about the methods Google needs to use to ensure that the ranking isn't rigged? There have always been recommendation systems with consequences for those being recommended – financial analysts picking stock market winners, for instance – but none so central to a space or activity as Google is to the Web.

Is privacy a private good or a public good? If an individual cedes his privacy, for example by keeping an explicit blog, is that a free choice of a sovereign individual, or a betrayal of an important principle? Do we have duties not to give our information away, in order not to weaken the idea that one's identity and personality should be inviolable? Should we refrain from using credit cards, joining loyalty schemes, using e-government websites? All of these constitute a semi-permanent record of our business.

There are no right or wrong answers, except to say that the study and science of the Web has to be deeply interdisciplinary, involving lawyers, technologists, sociologists, policing and security experts and philosophers reasoning and cooperating together to try to discern and understand the new world we are creating. The consequences of principles are important evidence in judging their fitness, and these can be very different online than offline; we may have to rethink our principles, although the basic premises of the arguments remain the same.

WHAT IS ON THE HORIZON?

Privacy often clashes with other values that we consider important. In particular, information that may erode our privacy could also promote efficiency. For instance, in many major cities, particularly in crowded Europe and Asia, traffic congestion is a serious and expensive problem. Lives are constantly put at risk, not only from the pollution that idling engines cause but also from delays in getting emergency services to their destinations. Knowing where cars are is clearly important for traffic control, and technology has a role to play. This is hardly science fiction – in 2006 a committee of Members of the European Parliament recommended adoption of the eCall in-car system which logs accidents and locates the nearest emergency vehicles, which they claimed could save 2,500 lives per year.[4] IntelliOne, an American company, has developed a traffic monitoring system that locates mobile phones in cars twice per second, from which it can work out how fast the car is travelling, and therefore where the traffic snarl-ups are. It can even tell the difference between a traffic jam and a red light.[5]

It is helpful for an organisation to know what information its employees need, and so monitoring the webpages that they download is useful. Similarly, monitoring emails via keywords is also valuable; particular queries can be sent to the people who can best deal with the problem. But do we really want our bosses to know what we are looking at, and reading our conversations?

Electronic tagging, of animals, children, property or criminals is becoming increasingly popular (for different reasons) in order to keep track of their whereabouts. But for the law-abiding, tagging could compromise privacy; taking the dog for a walk, going for a day out with the children or even carrying around tagged valuables would tell some sort of database where one is. The criminal is tagged to prevent the breaking of a curfew or condition of release, which is all very well, except that there may be a legitimate yet private purpose in travelling somewhere. The presumption that criminals forfeit *all* rights to privacy as a result of their crimes is a very harsh one unsupported in most jurisdictions. And suppose the crime in question was a political crime?

The information involved can be extremely mundane, but in the right context and the wrong hands very useful indeed. And it may be hard in advance to realise what potential there is for undermining privacy. You don't need supercomputers.

Our homes are host to many small, relatively stupid, relatively powerless computing devices, embedded in household goods. Such gadgets, linked together, can create surprisingly intelligent and flexible behaviour, to keep heating costs and environmental damage down, or to deploy resources intelligently to save money. Five minutes before it goes off, the alarm clock could send a message to the kettle to switch on, and the toilet seat and towel rail to warm up. Activating the shower might start the toaster. The coffee machine might sense when coffee had been poured and then send a message to the car ignition. In the car the seat belt might tell the garage door to open, while the garage door turns the central heating down. Nothing in that chain of systems is doing anything more complex than sensing things about their own use, and sending basic messages to other gizmos. Out of all that simple activity comes a sort of cleverness in the arrangement of the house.

Probably no-one would want an intelligent house; rather, the point is that information is being created that can be monitored, and the systems around you could be telling the world what is going on in your home. Domestic activity usually leaves little trace; snoopers are often reduced to relatively coarse methods of detection, such as scrabbling through litter bins. But a coffee machine that tells other household devices about itself could potentially be used to tell observers how many pots of coffee are made during the day, a much finer-grained detail of household life which, together with other details could be used to paint quite an accurate picture. Your coffee machine could be used to spy on you.

Computers are getting smaller and smaller, and can be made of, or fitted into, many new and interesting materials. The possibilities are endless, but so are the dangers. For instance, the field of electronic textiles or 'washable computing' provides all sorts of fascinating futures. Fabrics that can monitor vital signs, generate heat or act as switches suggest limitless possibilities, from the ridiculous – clothes that change colour constantly – to the useful – a jacket that recharges your mobile phone. Textronic's 'textro-polymer' is made of fibres that change their resistance as they are deformed or stretched, and so can detect pressure.[6] Very handy – but imagine a bedsheet that was able to detect, and broadcast, the number of people lying on it.

The information gathered by such devices has many important, interesting and genuinely useful purposes, and so they will continue to proliferate. But as they do, so will the dangers. The spy of the future will not be a shabby man with binoculars or a telephoto lens; tomorrow's spies will be coffee machines, bed linen and clothes.

And we shouldn't assume that we will spot the dangers in advance. If the short term benefits of technology are good enough, we tend not to question them. Had the government demanded that we all carry around electronic devices that broadcast our whereabouts to a central database, that the information should be stored there indefinitely, and that the police should be able to access it with relatively minimal oversight, there would have been an outcry. But in the real world most if not all of us carry such devices around voluntarily, in the shape of our mobile phones. The benefits, we generally reckon, outweigh the costs – which they probably do, but that is merely luck. Precautions against misuse were not discussed widely. We sleepwalked into the danger.

Crooks and nannies: crime and surveillance in the real world

This is all hypothetical so far; are there any specific examples of apparent threats to privacy from digital technologies? Here are a couple of instances where computing systems provide a new source of worry about our shrinking private space, one patently dangerous, the other less obviously so. Both examples were taken from a particular newspaper from a date late in 2005 chosen at random.

The first concerns identity theft. The article in question, sub-titled 'Privacy laws gain support in America, after a year of huge violations',[7] begins by drawing a disturbing analogy between the industrial revolution and our own IT-driven development.

In the industrial age, factories spewed out soot and sludge that polluted the environment; in the information age, companies leak data that can also expose the public to harm. When it came to pollution, politicians and even industrialists eventually agreed on the need for regulation to keep factories in check. This is now happening for privacy regulation in America.

Identity theft cost the US upwards of $50 billion a year as early as 2002. This has been an obvious danger for some years now, and the European Union, with its more careful, less swashbuckling politico-legal culture, has traditionally taken it much more seriously. Indeed, 1998 nearly saw a trade war break out between the US and the EU over the EU's supposedly over-Draconian privacy directive which demanded companies allow their customers to alter incorrect data held about them. But American business is now coming round to the European point of view.

What changed in the interim is the discovery of the size of the problem, but even that was something of an accident. California, more liberal and namby-pamby than most American states, pioneered a privacy law demanding that individuals had to be notified whenever a company discovered that data about those individuals had leaked. Until then, a company compromised by hackers did not have to inform anyone, not even victims or law-enforcement agents, of the breach. Opponents of the measure complained that it would create a bad environment for business, and businesses would flee for other states. What actually happened was that the law began to bite.

February 2005 saw ChoicePoint, a large data collection agency which holds nineteen billion records, 'fess up. It told 145,000 people that it had inadvertently given personal data away to fraudsters, including social security numbers (the basic identifier of the individual for the American government). Even then it waited five months after the discovery of the problem to inform those affected, of whom 750 had already spotted some fraudulent activity.[8] Later that month the Bank of America admitted it had lost data tapes with personal information about one million government employees, including some members of the Senate (this at least was accident and not fraud).[9] In June came the revelation that information about forty million credit card accounts had been stolen.[10] Small wonder that by the end of the year, businesses themselves were begging Congress to pass a federal privacy law.

Firms routinely collect more data than they need, keep it unencrypted and without even basic password protection, and for too long. Security is not the answer to this; it is of course necessary, but not sufficient. As privacy expert Charles Raab memorably put it:

> … it is no comfort to a privacy-aware individual to be told that inaccurate, outdated, excessive and irrelevant data about her are encrypted and stored behind hacker-proof firewalls until put to use by (say) a credit-granting organization in making decisions about her.[11]

The temptations for crooks are immense, because even though the data is potentially valuable in itself (which is why firms keep it), it has other uses. Most obviously, knowledge of credit card or bank details can be used to extract money from an account.

The scary part is that such data plays the extra and important role of identifying its subject. An identification system needs to pick on some aspect of an individual that will be very hard for other people to fake. Identity theft involves the thief extracting enough knowledge about the victim's confidential affairs to plausibly pass as the victim; the thief can then behave illegally or suspiciously, all the while understood by the system as being someone else. This is an inevitable consequence of, and made easier by, the disappearance of the body. Such illegal behaviour might not harm the victim directly; for example, a money launderer might open a bank account in a victim's name to deposit ill-gotten gains and withdraw them in a harder-to-trace form. Technically, such a scam actually makes the victim richer, at least temporarily.

Identify theft is a worry because it is comparatively hard to prove, as it is the victim's identity that is in question. Furthermore, the crime can happen without anyone being aware of it for a while; even something as basic as unauthorised use of credit card details may not be discovered until the thief bumps up against your credit limit, or you get your credit card bill some weeks later, in which time you or your bank could have lost an awful lot of money. Finally, because the behaviour that identity thieves indulge in reflects badly on you, you may gain a bad record or reputation as a result of the theft. You may find yourself inconveniently on a credit blacklist, or dangerously on an FBI wanted list, and yet it is hardly possible to check. Someone with a bad credit record can take years to regain their good name, while someone who is thought to be a terrorist might be blissfully unaware of the danger until they are surrounded at gunpoint by highly-trained agents at JFK Airport. At a time when law enforcement and habeas corpus measures are evolving rapidly as part of the War on

Terror, the end result might be weeks or even years in prison with precious few ways of establishing innocence. After all, it is not a case of proving that you are who you say you are; you have to prove that there is another person who has been masquerading as you, a much harder task.

Identity theft is a great concern to many people, and is a well-known example of what can happen when private data falls into the wrong hands. The invasion of privacy is the means to a criminal end: the main aim is something else, be it straightforward theft, money laundering, fraud, creating a disguise, illegal immigration, terrorism or what have you. But our second news story shows that the invasion of privacy may sometimes be exactly the point.

The rapidly greying population of Japan is trying to cope, technologically, with its demographic shift.[12] Average life expectancy, currently eighty-two, is growing by 2.5 years each decade while the Japanese birth rate is one of the smallest in the world. Add to that the Japanese aversion to immigration to produce the spectre of a society, in not many years' time, with an unusually large number of elderly citizens and relatively few younger people to provide care. The Japanese solution, we should not be surprised to hear, is to provide incredible techno-gadgets to take on some of the burden. The *Economist* highlights a number of products, of which three in particular are of interest to us.

Synclayer has a system with which elderly people can monitor vital signs such as blood pressure and temperature, and send them at a constant rate to the health services for automatic monitoring. Any indications of danger can then be acted upon immediately. Another system by Synclayer provides a sensor that detects particular movements, for instance, the opening of the fridge door.

Every time the elderly person opens his or her fridge, a message is sent over a Local Area Network (LAN) that the door has opened, and the time is stored in a database. Relatives or health workers can then monitor activity and check up if things are too quiet. Zojirushi, NTT DoCoMo and Fujitsu have developed the iPot, an electric kettle that keeps water hot all day for the making of tea or miso soup (and a gadget emphatically not to be confused with the marijuana-scented MP3 player[13]). Such kettles are common in Japan, but this one transmits a message to a server by wireless whenever the kettle is used, and a twice-daily report is sent to a designated mobile phone or email address of a relative or carer.

The Spy in the Coffee Machine was chosen as the title of this book, based on the coffee machine scenario from the previous section, as used in an invited talk given by one of the present authors. The scenario was technologically plausible, if perhaps unlikely as a serious attempt to invade privacy. Yet while we were pitching the proposal to Oneworld publishers, something very similar was actually reaching the market. Of course, the iPot is an extremely creative solution to a serious problem, and the invasion of the privacy of the elderly people involved will be with their permission. The information gathered will be used for their benefit; if they are incapacitated for any reason, then their inactivity should be detectable within a few hours, which may make the difference between life and death. We certainly do not wish to suggest Synclayer or Zojirushi have sinister intentions.

But look at the technology to monitor mundane activity. Tiny computers and sensors, wireless networks and the Internet all come together to enable information about making coffee or opening the fridge to be transferred instantly to a remote observer, who need not even be in the same country.

And it should not be assumed that one can merely avoid using such applications. One can, of course, not allow one's carers to install an iPot. But so effective is miniaturisation that one can be spied upon by all sorts of people in all sorts of ways. For instance, in the United Kingdom, microchips capable of assessing the weight of rubbish have been fitted to thousands of the wheelie bins that are used to store household waste before it is picked up by dustcarts run by local councils. A number of councils have distributed bins that can transmit information to a central database about the disposal practices of individual families. The chips are fitted to the lip of the bin and scanned as the bin is tipped into the dustcart. In theory, the idea is to monitor the number of bins that dustmen have emptied, and to judge disputes between neighbours. But if the dustcart also contains weighing equipment (and some do), then the weight of rubbish disposed of could be linked to an individual household.[14]

When the story broke, some raised civil liberties concerns, but they have to be balanced against monitoring waste disposal and improving Britain's poor recycling record. Health care, the environment and, of course, security against crime and terrorism are perennial reasons for introducing privacy-invading technology. It is extremely difficult for someone to evade this sort of monitoring. Merely residing in South Norfolk or St Helens makes you liable to be snooped on by your own bin.

THE THREAT OF THE DIGITAL

Why do digital technologies in particular threaten privacy? Much has to do with the ways that information is represented, and how it is communicated. Digital information lasts a long time, effectively forever if it is periodically copied, backed up and stored using up-to-date formats. Copying is simple and accurate, and transfer from one person to another trivial. Searching through digital information is fast; discovering a tiny number of references to a person in a large database, virtually impossible to spot with the human eye, is a simple matter with a computer. Information that is harmless on its own can be placed in significant new contexts. While from the subject's point of view, it is hard to know when privacy has been breached, harder still to determine who is responsible, and there is no central authority from which to obtain redress.

Meanwhile, with its distributed structure and cleverly-designed architecture, the World Wide Web is rapidly becoming the information repository of choice. This increases risk as it brings together under one virtual roof more information about you than other more traditional repositories. It is possible to build up a very comprehensive picture of you from your web presence. And for some reason that sociologists would be more qualified to address, the Web attracts many types of subterranean behaviour. The tendency of people to publish compromising material, or to engage in risky behaviour, seems, anecdotally at least, highly prevalent online.

Compare the digital with other more usual methods of transferring private information. *Paper* is bulky, hard to copy and copying is not always accurate. Comprehensive information about oneself is not usually stored in one physical document. *Human memory* is notoriously fallible, and hard to transfer – it usually involves the time-consuming representation of the memory before the transfer can begin, so even if the memory is accurate the representation of it may not be. *Gossip* is hard to suppress – it has been compared to the many-headed hydra of Greek myth, in that whenever one head it chopped off, two more grow in its place. However it is typically inaccurate, at least after a relatively small number of transfers between people (not that the inaccuracy seems to bother them), and it can be hard to find the gossip you need to order – it is supply- rather than demand-driven. The transfer of digital information is far more powerful.

Privacies

The assiduous reader will have noted that privacy has not been defined – we have talked about threats to it and invasions of it, not about what would be or is being invaded. But privacy is a many-splendoured thing, as we will see in this book. A dictionary definition won't quite nail the topic down as we would like.

The usual understanding of privacy is to do with a subject's control of information about him or herself. Knowledge about a person is often made into a document such as a medical record or a photograph. If the person has a measure of privacy, then it is possible to restrict the distribution of the representation of that knowledge.

Information about a person could, of course, be false, out of date or badly maintained, or because of a simple error such as a confusion of names it might be thought to apply to the wrong person. Information can be used to restrict someone's freedom of action, again either intentionally or otherwise. Someone could be coerced into behaving in a particular way with a threat to release certain information, or someone's choices could be diminished.

Animal rights activists have been known to release personal information to intimidate opponents.[15] In a number of cultures publicity about HIV status, homosexuality, or illegitimacy can result in social stigma. In the Soviet Union, someone's family background or party membership could determine their official status.[16] Politicians live under the constant threat of the effect of the information about them.

But privacy is not straightforwardly definable in simple terms of access and control of information. One has private spaces, takes private decisions, has freedom of thought, has private property – and all of these have online analogues. When cameras became quick enough to allow photographs to be taken without an elaborate pose, a new issue arose as to whether people – public figures, perhaps – had any kind of right to prevent others taking a likeness without consent, even in a public place. One can't step into a public place without expecting to be *seen*, but the recording of that moment is an entirely different matter. There are many cultures which lack the assumption that one cannot be private in a public place; it is a Western dogma that one's privacy cannot be invaded if one is voluntarily in public.

Privacy takes a number of shapes, and can manifest itself in several different ways. One's house is a literal private space, where one would hope to control access. One's body is private; naturally one would want to restrict others' physical access to it, but also one often wishes to avoid even being seen. Many people wish to keep knowledge about themselves private, sometimes for pragmatic reasons (bank details), but sometimes for reasons that are less tangible (salary). For some, privacy is an absence of people. For others, it is about carving a small, controllable space out of a wider untamed one. Others wish to avoid interference with their decisions, or do not want to be held accountable for some of their acts. Still others want to be free to exchange their property. Some wish to subvert society without risking punishment.

Our second reason for being wary of definitions is that privacy is not value-neutral. It is not an unalloyed good, although much privacy discourse assumes it is. Some people and some cultures regard privacy with suspicion. Most of us at one time or another seek privacy, but at other times shun it without inconsistency. In general, in the West at least, the popular opinion of privacy has become more positive over the centuries. Privacy is (beginning to be) protected by the law, and many social trends take us in the direction of greater privacy, such as the reduction in the size of families living in a single household. But on the other hand, many use new technologies to expose themselves to view to a previously unimaginable degree. Webcams and *Big Brother* provide almost unlimited access to some exhibitionists, while very few people will pass up the opportunity to appear on television. Television hosts such as Jerry Springer base careers on the willingness of bizarre and damaged people to wash their dirty linen in public. Even very recently bereaved people will talk about their loss on TV news programmes. Most academics would kill to be interviewed about their work, even as they cling tenaciously to the copyrights on their unread articles. Many diaries are written to be read (ultimately). As Wilde put it, 'there is only one thing in the world worse than being talked about, and that is *not* being talked about.'

This ambivalence about publicity and privacy dates back to the key founding moments of Western civilisation. For instance, Plato, in his *Republic*, imagined a society where the children of the ruling class would be educated in common and quarantined from the usual family life. Meanwhile, Aristotle's *Politics* makes a modern-sounding distinction between the private domain of the household and the public space of the *polis*, the democratic decision-making forum where all citizens' voices were heard. But Aristotle's view was that the private domain was uninteresting and dull – boring household governance – whereas the *polis* was where it was at. This preference for the public was preserved by etymology – the word 'private' is related to Latin 'privare', to deprive, and the connotation of privacy for classical thinkers was very much to do with deprivation rather than voluntary withdrawal.

A third privacy-related dilemma is that it benefits different agents. If you wish something you do to be unknown to the rest of society, then you are the beneficiary of your privacy. On the other hand, if you wish to do something that many consider disgusting, such as urination, in public, then you will be admonished that that is an action that should only occur in private, and in that case your (enforced) privacy benefits everybody else, and may in fact frustrate your reasonable or unreasonable exhibitionism (it is only a couple of centuries since seeing a monarch 'at his stool' was considered a great privilege). Sometimes privacy is a space into which one can gratefully withdraw, sometimes it is the space where one is corralled to prevent offence. One can be either comforted or frustrated by decorum. Feminist thinkers have complained that the privacy of 'one's own home' facilitates a great deal of abuse of wives and children by husbands, and entrenches patriarchy.[17]

Privacy can also be aggregated. Groups can benefit from privacy (families, say) without necessarily everyone within the group benefiting (downtrodden wives). Within a group one can be both private and not private; one can be private from the outside world, yet visible and accessible to others in the group. Even within a private group, one can require privacy – many people seek privacy away from their family, even when they are already within the paradigm private space, their own home.

Fourthly, privacy is very similar to a number of other concepts, and is hard to disentangle. For instance, there are strong connections between privacy and secrecy, but we should not confuse them. A state secret is secret but not private; one's clothes are private but not secret. Those who conceive of privacy as a lack of accountability merely want to make their own decisions about, for instance, marriage or money or the way they manage their children without interference – they are not necessarily bothered about who knows about them. Structurally, there is very little distinction between privacy and loneliness, or ostracism, or deprivation, or isolation. The difference may well be the attitude we hold towards the private state, rather than any structures or external relations for the subject. Privacy often carries with it a notion of choice. One chooses to be private, whereas one does not (usually) choose to be lonely.

For all these reasons, we are wary of defining privacy, because it would be hard – we suspect impossible – to give necessary and sufficient conditions, especially as technology changes the context so rapidly. This book, focusing on technology in twenty-first century Western democracies is certainly not going to attempt to nail down such a slippery concept. Nevertheless, it is well to note that any concept whose definition and properties are tightly interwoven with social practice has a cultural location and a history, and we must expect that the concept will change with the context.

One final caveat: it is quite clear that many people wish to obtain or preserve privacy because they are performing actions that are illegal or otherwise damaging to others. Similarly, many people, organisations or authorities wish to invade privacy for profit or political gain, whatever rights they trample upon. Such cases of transgression of the law or accepted moral codes are pretty straightforward to judge (if hard to prevent in practice), and we do not wish to focus upon them. The point about privacy is that it raises *hard* cases; people want privacy for perfectly good reasons, and others want information for equally good reasons. Technology will alter the delicate balance between such people as it evolves. In this book we are interested, primarily, in how to prioritise dealings made in perfectly good faith. When most people are law-abiding and public-spirited, how do we avoid risk, and how should we prevent illegal actions in the future without demonising those in the present?

CASE STUDY: FROM CASH TO E-CASH

One of the most prominent examples of the adoption of a digital technology undermining our privacy is the shift from anonymous cash to electronic money in the world economy. More people are using cards for large sums of money, and new methods are being developed which are practical for small transactions. It is highly unlikely that cash will disappear in the foreseeable future, but we may well see less of it; it will be quite possible to live without cash, and there may even be a premium to use it if it becomes more expensive to process. But this affects our anonymity. Only a few decades ago, the passage of notes was rare enough to allow the noting down of serial numbers to facilitate tracing. This is impractical today, except when a note can be traced to a batch of new notes with consecutive numbers. Nowadays, once a coin or note has been passed on, there is nothing tangible to connect you with it. Electronic forms of money, however, leave trails behind; nothing electronic can replicate the anonymity of handing over a physical object.

Almost any exchange of resources in which you take part could involve your leaving behind a characteristic trail for anyone to follow. The last movements of the September 11 hijackers were easily traceable by their spending patterns. This, of course, did not help with prevention, but is of enormous importance in assembling evidence of criminal activity after the fact. Furthermore, observation of the pattern of spending can help in tracing a stolen card, if the character, frequency and size of one's purchases suddenly change.

2

THE SURVEILLANCE SOCIETY

FROM HABIT TO INSTINCT

> There was of course no way of knowing whether you were
> being watched at any given moment. How often, or on what
> system, the Thought Police plugged in on any individual wire
> was guesswork. It was even conceivable that they watched
> everybody all the time. But at any rate they could plug into your
> wire whenever they wanted to. You had to live – did live, from
> habit that became instinct – in the assumption that every sound
> you made was overheard, and, except in darkness, every move-
> ment scrutinized.[18]

Thus Big Brother achieved total control in *Nineteen Eighty-Four*,
through a combination of certainty and uncertainty. Winston
Smith had to be certain that the infrastructure was in place, but, as
Richard Posner points out, it is unlikely there would be sufficient
manpower to watch everybody all the time.[19] Hence, to minimise
its costs, the system also needed uncertainty – one could calculate
the likelihood that one was being observed, but the probability
should never reach zero. That likelihood had also to be balanced
against the penalties. If a totalitarian regime wishes to exercise
control, it needs to apply severe sanctions in order to weight the
calculations in its favour. Examples need to be made, such as the

four year sentence given to Abdel-Karim Nabil Suleiman, an Egyptian blogger, for insulting Islam,[20] or the long prison terms handed out in China to dissidents and webmasters deemed to have gone too far in criticising the government.[21]

In countries where political freedom is taken seriously, people can afford to be more relaxed about surveillance. Nonetheless Western democracies are now fully-fledged 'surveillance societies', to use the words of a recent report for the UK's Information Commissioner,[22] a description endorsed by 79% of British adults in a poll of November 2006.[23] Surveillance is defined as attention to information about people that is *purposeful*, *routine*, *systematic* and *focused*, and in surveillance societies is used for control, entitlement, management, influence and protection.[24] This is not to suggest that this dramatic situation is necessarily sinister. It may well be that there is a general social gain from such surveillance.

But there are still risks, however benign the intent. Information can be misused, and governments can make mistakes. As one of the present authors said in an earlier publication,

> Attempts to complain about … intrusion are standardly met by the stunningly false reply that 'if you keep within the law, you have nothing to fear'. A response that would be correct, but somewhat less persuasive, would be 'if you keep within the law, and the government keeps within the law, and its employees keep within the law, and the computer holding the database doesn't screw up, and the system is carefully designed according to well-understood software engineering principles and maintained properly, and the government doesn't scrimp on the outlay, and all the data are entered carefully, and the police are adequately trained to use the system, and the

system isn't hacked into, and your identity isn't stolen, and the local hardware functions well, you have nothing to fear.'[25]

In one notorious incident, a Canadian software engineer of Syrian origin, Maher Arar, was detained by American immigration during a stopover in the US on the basis of false information provided about him by the Royal Canadian Mounted Police, and deported to Syria under the covert scheme for extraordinary rendition. He spent nearly a year in a Syrian jail under torture. Some years later he extracted an apology and C$10.5 million from the Canadian government. At the time of writing, the Americans have not admitted any liability.

Such horror stories are rare, but they fuel privacy activism. For most of us, surveillance is tedious but part and parcel of everyday life, whether travelling, shopping, at school, in the hospital or even sitting at home.[26] When anti-surveillance activists complain, what results is as often bathos as genuine fear of the Thought Police.

> Until [11 September 2001] I had always carried my small Swiss knife with me on trips just in case I needed one of the handy gadgets, like the tiny screwdriver for my glasses. I had nothing to hide. But when [after the terrorists' attack] I eventually managed to board a flight back home to Kingston, Ontario, my knife had to travel separately in an airport security envelope. There was also something unnerving about running the gauntlet of armed guards and military personnel as I made my way through the long security lines in the airport at Toronto. There was something to fear, even though, as a white male, I was not singled out for special security. As we all have discovered since, this was only the beginning.

Since then I have had my face scrutinized by intelligent cameras at Keflavik Airport in Iceland, and I have been warned of increased security because of terrorist threats by the bright new display units at Narita Airport in Tokyo. I have experienced new surveillance measures in global cities like London, Sydney, and Vienna (dogs checking carry-on at the gate), and right now I happen to be writing these words in the departure lounge at Logan Airport, Boston, from which two of those fated flights departed in September 2001. Scrutiny of baggage and of persons, from check-in to the entry ramp, is much more rigorous. I have to start up my laptop for the security guards, and show my passport photo before boarding. Airlines entering the USA are obliged to send passenger data to the destination in advance. As routine practices, all this is new.[27]

The harm reported here doesn't seem very great, in the context of the appalling events which prompted the worldwide security upgrade. When John Stuart Mill railed against tyranny, he was probably considering inconveniences more major than being cruelly prevented from tightening the screw on his spectacles. Given his air miles, the author's massive carbon footprint is probably the bigger threat to humanity. The complaint here is about the fact of surveillance, not its consequences.

Security, social cohesion, health, the environment

When the prophetic but currently unfashionable Marshall McLuhan predicted that we would soon be living in a global village thanks to new technologies and media, most people took that to mean that travel would be straightforward, intermingling of diverse cultures frequent and influences wide and strong. But one other property of a village is the absence of anonymity and secrecy. Privacy is at a premium, and that is another aspect of the global village with which we will have to come to terms.

In fact, it does seem that most people live reasonably and happily with surveillance systems in place, and adapt themselves by habit to the new environment. Privacy and anonymity are to an extent modern inventions and ideals, and many prefer to lay stress on security and cohesion. Even as our modern Western concepts of privacy were being forged by thinkers such as Locke, Smith and Mill,[28] the spirit of the Enlightenment was sceptical about privacy as a value; many writers and thinkers were nervous that greater privacy would promote dissembling and hypocrisy, and allow 'uncivilised' behaviour or lack of self-control.[29]

In a survey in 2002, the Pew Global Attitudes Project discovered widespread fear of crime and terrorism. Of the several countries surveyed, only in Jordan, Canada, South Korea and China did 40% or fewer of the population say that crime was a 'very big' problem. 48% of Americans, 61% of Britons, 69% of Turks, 76% of the French, 80% of Poles, 86% of Indians, 93% of Guatemalans, 96% of Bangladeshis and 96% of South Africans were seriously worried by crime. In most countries more than half of the population worried about terrorism, while some countries with particularly low scores (the UK, 23%, and Jordan, 15%) have since suffered drastically at the hands of terrorists.[30]

It is quite likely that the airport security measures mentioned above prevented few terror attacks (probably none). But of course the *absence* of at least some of them allowed the September 11 attacks to take place. It was the use of tiny knives and other sharp objects that enabled the terrorists to gain control of the four aircraft, for instance. Of course these things are harmless in the hands of most people, and even putting an aircraft into the control of hijackers would not normally endanger it. The events of September 11 changed our understanding of the risks.

The War on Terror that followed is understood by its protagonists (on both sides) as a robust defence of liberalism against a particular set of readings of Islam. The dilemma liberals face is that tolerating intolerance is a weakness of a tolerant society.[31] If intolerance is relatively harmless, and affects few individuals, then the liberal can tolerate the intolerant. But when intolerant people start to murder those they do not tolerate, intolerance becomes something to address, not to tolerate. This line of thought, if justified, allows liberals to take measures to read others' emails, put them under surveillance, discourage their political activities and so on.

Security is a prominent example of the sort of value that can compete with privacy. Police forces the world over have privacy-invading powers, from surveillance to rights to imprison. Only very extreme liberals believe that one can have freedom independently of a functioning society that gives actions meaning. It follows that such a society is a precursor to all free action, and therefore it is essential to protect it.

Measures to support social cohesion are obviously more valuable in societies that do not cohere very well naturally. One reason why the ghastly Taliban were initially welcomed in Afghanistan was that they at least had the muscle to beat back various feuding warlords, and were religious and moral enough to rule fairly – even if that rule was harsh and justice rarely tempered with mercy. Some social cohesion was judged by many Afghans as being better than none.

Other societies – often Asian ones – value cohesion as an end in itself. It is also often argued, and again Asia is a case in point, that government is more effective with reliable data. These ideas also tend to reduce the space for private action.

Another area to benefit from surveillance is the management of public health problems. For instance, in Singapore in 2003, the dangers of the SARS outbreak were taken extremely seriously, partly because of the natural virulence of the disease, and partly because of the density of population in that island state. The government imposed a quarantine on people who had been in contact with those diagnosed with SARS, but of course the combinatorial explosion of the numbers affected by the scheme soon overwhelmed the Ministry of Health's information systems, both in terms of administering the quarantine and tracking down those who had been in contact with sufferers. In the end a redesigned information system covering several ministries was created at short notice by an agency of the Ministry of Defence integrating contact tracing, epidemiology, disease control, front-line operations, and provision of leave of absence during quarantine in a single surveillance architecture. The imposition on civil liberties was high, but SARS was stamped out in Singapore within weeks.[32]

And surveillance can help with our understanding of the environment and our relationship with it. The attacks of September 11 have been on our minds in this chapter, but following the collapse of the twin towers and evaluation of the escape and rescue procedures, the US National Institute of Standards and Technology's report on the disaster recommended improved and widespread provision of CCTV cameras to allow the location and responses of people to be monitored in the event of a calamity, thereby allowing emergency services to coordinate and revise their efforts in real time.

In short, the development of surveillance has not gone the way predicted by Orwell. It has been a rational process, a response to the demands of capitalism and the growth of the modern nation state (though the roles of the Cold War and the War on Terror should not be underplayed). The chief aim has been efficient administration, not the preservation of power by elites. That said, one highly unfortunate side effect of the drive to efficiency in the Western capitalist democracies is that surveillance techniques have been developed that can be, and often are, exported to somewhat less liberal places.

IS PRIVACY A GOOD THING?

If all that about efficient government and security is true, why do we need privacy at all? The high value of privacy has become something of a dogma, and needs, like all dogmas, to be questioned. There are indeed many good reasons to value it.

In the first place, it is strongly associated with intimacy and intimate relations. As the demand for intimacy is strong, sufficient private space to enjoy relations of love, familial intimacy and friendship is desirable. Even in the workplace, a private space is needed to support people in their work; it is hard to work in public. Sociologist Erving Goffman reminds us of how much goes on beyond the public gaze.

> The backstage language consists of reciprocal first-naming, co-operative decision-making, profanity, open sexual remarks, elaborate griping, smoking, rough informal dress, "sloppy"

sitting and standing posture, use of dialect or sub-standard speech, mumbling and shouting, playful aggression and "kidding," inconsiderateness for the other in minor but potentially symbolic acts, minor physical self-involvements such as humming, whistling, chewing, nibbling, belching and flatulence.[33]

But liberalism has taken the idea of the centrality of privacy much further. Privacy first reached prominence in a famous review by Samuel Warren and Louis Brandeis, who analysed the American constitution and its amendments – in which the word 'privacy' hardly occurs – and derived a right to privacy from other more explicit rights. Nevertheless they claimed that privacy was not *reducible* to other rights.

The legalistic niceties of the constitution are of course beyond our expertise and the scope of this book. But the question of whether privacy is reducible to another value is an important piece of context for our thinking about it. If the reason that we want privacy is grounded in *another* value or set of values, then the protection of those other values seems to be something more basic than the protection of privacy. Philosopher Judith Jarvis Thompson has argued that privacy is such a heterogeneous concept that it is impossible to imagine how a single right could cover all the cases it would be applied to. So different are the various aspects of privacy, that we cannot say that 'all cases of privacy are reducible to *this* particular more basic right'. In different contexts, different basic rights will be evoked.[34] However, as was pointed out immediately in response, some of the 'rights' she claims as more basic than privacy seem a lot less straightforward and intuitive – such as the right not to be looked at.[35] It seems much more intuitive to say that we have a right to privacy from which we derive our preference about being looked at. As Goffman argued, there does seem to be a general human need for some limits to scrutiny.

In more general terms, privacy is strongly connected to *autonomy*,[36] the idea that no-one should interfere with what one does (as far as possible). If one is to be free, one needs to be able to act without interference, and to do that it is necessary to control one's environment in certain ways. One has to be able, if needs be, to prevent others from knowing certain things about one, from entering one's private space, or from countermanding one's decisions.

The original argument for this goes back to the great liberal thinker John Stuart Mill, who argued that society was able to apply so much pressure to the citizen that he could be prevented from working out what he wanted to do, and whether it was morally justified.[37] Consequently, the citizen needed protection against unwarranted interference, and that protection is what we call privacy. Privacy is necessary for people to become properly moral thinkers and persons. We need to *reflect* on the things we want to do and ought to do, and the space for reflection is typically private. We need to *control* the amount of access others have to us, because we need to be aware that we are following our own preferences, not those that others have imposed on us.[38]

Ultimately therefore, privacy is a matter of respect for persons. If we are to treat others as inviolable, then it follows that we must give them private spaces of various types. We need to allow them physical locations where they can escape surveillance, restrict the flow of information about them, and prevent unwarranted interference in their decisions. We might debate the limits of these spaces, but if people are intrinsically valuable such spaces must be available to them.

PRIVACY AND THE LAW

In the absence of effective social sanction, the law is often invoked. A society or culture can't make a technology like the Web disappear. People from conservative cultures like China's might disapprove of bloggers such as Mu Zumei, whose sex blog received hundreds of thousands of visits, but there is little to be done informally. On the other hand, the Chinese *authorities* can monitor, close down or even arrest bloggers who incur their displeasure.[39] Given that the Chinese government wishes to benefit from the Internet, it will have to tolerate the existence of the blogosphere; it can't get rid of all blogs, no matter how hard it tries, without fatally undermining the Internet's infrastructure. But it can come down very hard indeed on individual bloggers. Such political and legal sanction is an important variable in the relation between technology and society.

Governments focus on the harms that new technologies bring in their wake, perhaps naturally since it is the harms that tend to come to attention first. People complain early and hard about changes they don't like; at various times there have been deep and heartfelt worries about the waltz, non-representative art, jazz, hula hoops and mobile phones. Over time, some if not all of these worries are shown to be exaggerated or irrelevant. In the meantime early legislation can stifle a technology (something of this sort seems to be happening with stem cell research in some countries[40]).

On the other hand, the harms are offset with benefits which are much less tangible, harder to quantify and difficult to notice since they arrive gradually across a society over a period of years. Furthermore, many technologies rely on network effects, which means that early adopters get relatively few benefits, and it is only when a critical mass of users arrives that the full benefits are realised (a phone network is of much greater value when it has a lot of users – Alexander Graham Bell, pioneer that he was, had far fewer interesting phone conversations than we do).

Technologies don't fundamentally change the politics of society and interaction,[41] but they do change the social conditions of those interactions. Freedom of speech is freedom of speech, but a digital technology is an entirely new context in which such freedom can be exercised. Hence it is not the novelty of the technology that is the focus, so much as the novelty of the context it provides.[42] As Warren and Brandeis put it, a new context can often require a rethink of our rights.

> Recent inventions and business methods call attention to the next step which must be taken for the protection of the person, and for securing … the right "to be let alone." Instantaneous photographs and newspaper enterprise have invaded the sacred precincts of private and domestic life; and numerous mechanical devices threaten to make good the prediction that "what is whispered in the closet shall be proclaimed from the house-tops." For years there has been a feeling that the law must afford some remedy for the unauthorized circulation of portraits of private persons; and the evil of invasion of privacy by the newspapers [has been] long keenly felt ….[43]

As they point out, in the mid-nineteenth century virtually all privacy issues in the US could be worked out in court under contract law, because virtually all perceived betrayals of trust involved some kind of breach of contractual relations. Before the mobile camera, one had to sit consciously for a photograph to be taken, and so 'the law of contract or of trust might afford the prudent man sufficient safeguards against the improper circulation of his portrait'. But when one could be photographed without one's knowledge or consent, contract and trust ceased to be factors, and the aggrieved would have to reach for the law of tort instead.[44] The social benefits of mobile photography were clearly great enough that banning it would be counterproductive[45] (and unconstitutional), so instead the law had to evolve with the technology, infrastructure and institutions of society. If a society is to remain entrepreneurial and innovative, the law must change along with the context. This is the dilemma that the Chinese government faces as it tries to harness the economic benefits of the Internet without the corresponding political risks to one-party totalitarian rule.

An error often made by the promoters of surveillance technology is to assume that the uses of such technologies can be defined and limited in advance. On the classic model of bureaucratic rationality leading to surveillance and efficiency, originating with sociologist Max Weber, systems are set up for specific purposes anticipating instrumental gain. In that case, say the optimists, the system can be legitimised by legislation which sets out the circumstances in which it can be used; any further use of the system, or use of the information gleaned by the system, would therefore be ruled out by the enabling legislation in the first place. However, bureaucracies are very information-thirsty, which leads to what is popularly-known as 'function creep'.[46] A big store of information is simply too tempting for a bureaucracy to leave alone (after all, bureaucrats and their managers are judged by performance targets, and they surely can't be blamed as individuals for using whatever tools are to hand to meet them), and the legislative safeguards are generally inadequate (particularly in a common law jurisdiction such as the United Kingdom or the United States). A government could stretch the definition of legal use of the information, hoping ultimately to provoke a challenge in the courts which would allow a redefinition of the legal precedents. Often, laws governing information use are regulations which can be changed by statutory instruments or delegated legislation over which Parliamentary scrutiny is limited. And of course in countries with a large government majority and a strong system of party whipping, Parliamentary scrutiny of very detailed issues may not be terribly effective anyway.

It cannot be said that privacy is either being rolled back relentlessly or defended tenaciously: the position is patchy. It does not seem either that overweening government is taking our liberties away, or that data protection laws are 'over-zealous', in the words of Tony Blair.[47] Governments can't always get away with whatever they wish. The Terrorist Intervention and Protection System (TIPS), an American attempt to enlist people who had routine access to others' homes (e.g. mailmen, phone company employees) into the surveillance effort, had to be scaled back after a popular outcry:[48] the *vox populi* can be effective.

Into the constant battle between hawks and doves come singularities, unpredictable public events and scandals, and the media reporting of them. These singularities provoke public reaction which can be fierce or mild, and which tilt the debate suddenly, though not necessarily permanently, in one direction or another. A terrorist outrage or a prominent crime is likely to increase support for surveillance in the short term, while a very egregious misuse of information will do the opposite. Pollsters, who are as keen to be topical as other media analysts, often carry out polls in the immediate aftermath of a singularity, and so provide only a snapshot of a dynamic and unstable position that will be of little value only a few weeks later.

Sometimes spin trumps serious debate. The American Total Information Awareness system was intended to develop and integrate a number of surveillance programmes; of course its name is very misleading. 'Total' implies it will be information about everyone and everything; 'awareness' implies that there is someone taking notice of all the information rolling in. The name as a whole implies a single mind sifting information about everyone. That is scary, and there was an outcry.[49] The name was changed to *Terrorism* Information Awareness. With this new name, 'awareness' is good (though equally false), because the subjects of the programme are 'terrorists', who are feared by voters. Even better, they aren't voters themselves. A voter, not a terrorist, knows that he has never, and would never, plant a bomb to change the political make-up of a society, and so feels safe from the TIA system's scrutiny. How comforting a name can be.

CASE STUDY: ID CARDS IN THE UNITED KINGDOM

In Britain there has been a debate about whether to implement a system of identity cards for some years, during which both major parties have changed their views. Opposition parties face no Weberian pressures to make the bureaucracy function more efficiently, so it is more usual to see a government in favour.

Identity cards make an interesting example of the myriad and complex interactions between the state, citizenry, outside world, political forces and technology. The scheme in the United Kingdom to impose identity cards has often been justified by pointing out that many perfectly respectable Western democracies have ID cards, including 11 EU member states. In innocuous Belgium, it is compulsory to carry the card at all times, while Germany, Spain and Luxembourg insist residents must carry some form of identity document sufficient to establish identity to the police, although that document need not be their compulsory ID card.

But this argument misses the point. If we examine the specific circumstances of some of those ID schemes, we find significant differences traceable back to the unique histories and cultures of individual nations. For instance, the UK is a country that still uses the common law, built up by precedent rather than by legislative fiat. In a common law jurisdiction, the assumption is that citizens are free to do whatever they like unless there is a law against it. This means, among other things, that there is no canonical relationship between the citizen and the state, and that the idea of a single identity defined for each person and mapped onto a large centrally-held database would do violence to many British presumptions about the individual. In particular, there is nothing in law to prevent an individual using a number of different identities or aliases, rather as one can do online.

As a result of such considerations, recent proposals to introduce ID cards in the common law jurisdictions of Australia, New Zealand, the US and Canada have all failed in the face of objections from overwhelming numbers of people. However, for specific purposes they do have cards or other information-bearing tokens which serve to identify people in particular sectors, the most famous being the American Social Security number (SSN), created under President F.D. Roosevelt as an identifier for the social security system, but now used for a wide range of purposes, including as an identifier in the US military and for the Internal Revenue service. It is a nine-digit number issued to all citizens, and permanent and temporary (working) residents, and so is of relatively low integrity (there can only be one billion numbers issued before repetition would have to begin, and the current US population is around 300 million). There is no connection to a biometric database and so no way of ensuring that someone who presents an SSN is the person who is identified by it. That low integrity is a problem, as the SSN is used as an authenticator in many transactions, including opening bank accounts and other financial interactions. In the UK the driving licence is often used as a de facto ID card. This, incidentally, is function creep in action: an identifier for social security or driving licences develops a wider spread of uses.

It is extremely interesting to see the lack of homogeneity across the 100 countries with a national ID card system. Very few schemes were developed by democracies in peacetime (Holland

and Malaysia are exceptions); the overwhelming majority are legacies of either wartime measures (including Luxembourg), previous dictatorships (including Germany and Spain), or colonial
rule. This means that there are hardly any precedents of schemes
set up in order to solve specific problems, and which have sur-
vived a dose of democratic debate. Rather, most ID schemes,
being legacy systems, were simply retained, with the inertia of
pre-existence replacing constructive debate, and then adapted to
whatever purpose seemed appropriate at the time, be it tackling
crime, terrorism or illegal immigration, doling out benefits or
simplifying the interface between citizen and state.[50]

Ad hoc use and function creep are endemic to the field. The
UK has twice introduced (and repealed) ID card schemes, each of
which was a wartime measure for specific purposes. The National
Registration Act of 1915 required everyone between the ages of
15 and 65 to enrol on a national register in order to ensure the
workforce was used to best effect. The opposition Labour Party
demanded, and received, reassurance from the government that
the register would not be used to aid conscription. The Act also
included no requirement to carry the identity certificate or produce it on demand. Of course, the register was used when conscription was introduced, and by the end of the war the police
were empowered to see one's certificate on demand. The 1915
Act expired automatically when the war ended in late 1918.[51]

The Emergency Registration Act of 1939 introduced a card at
the outbreak of the Second World War, in order (i) to help with
the administration of mobilisation and mass evacuation, (ii) to
help administer rationing, and (iii) to provide necessary demographic statistics (the previous census had been in 1931, and the
next one scheduled, in 1941, could not be guaranteed to take place

in wartime conditions – in fact the 1931 census was destroyed in the war). Again the measure was popular at the time, but used beyond its original purpose and design – when it was abolished, to great applause, in 1952, it was being used for 32 purposes.[52]

Support for ID cards is positive, with 50% of people in favour in a poll of November 2006, and 39% against (though only 41% are fairly or very happy to have their own details on the register, against 52% who are fairly or very unhappy).[53] Indeed, the Home Office has been upbeat enough about the proposal to coin a cheery and cheesy slogan 'Everyone's unique. Let's keep it that way'.[54] The Identity Cards Act 2006 sets out a framework for rolling out a scheme, but is hazy about the details. In part this is for the sensible reason that the technology is developing all the time, although the Parliamentary Home Affairs Select Committee was right to be concerned that those details were 'a decision of the same order of importance as the architecture of the database'.[55]

The card itself is unlikely to use an RFID chip (see chapter 8), as with new US passports, but is likely to be the size of a credit card with a photograph and some biometric data. Information about one could be stored on the card in two ways: it could be printed legibly on the card (the government has hinted that this human-readable information would be more or less what is currently on a passport), or it could be encoded into a chip. Information would not need to be stored on a card – most of the registered information would be stored on a database linked to a National Identity Register, while the card would store a key which would link up with one's unique database entry. The likely biometrics used would be iris scans or fingerprints (the card owner would have to travel to a centre that was able to take a biometric measurement and add it to the National Identity Register), but much will depend on cost, practicality, anticipated harms of false positives or negatives, and the question of whether the aim of the biometric will be to confirm the identity of an individual (matching the biometric against a single entry in the database), or to identify an individual from a group (matching against a series of entries).

According to the Act, there are two statutory purposes for which the Register will be maintained (and it cannot be maintained for any other purpose):[56] the provision of a convenient method of identification of oneself to others who might reasonably require proof of identity, and of ascertaining whether someone is who they say they are if that is necessary in the public interest[57] (defined as national security, prevention or detection of crime, enforcement of immigration controls, enforcement of labour laws, and the securing of efficient provision of public services).[58]

Many of the definitions in the Identity Cards Act are very broad, and the chief safeguard is a number of assurances by Home Office ministers that they will be implemented and interpreted narrowly. No-one doubts that this is the current intention, and indeed it may well be that judges, when the Act is tested in court, will use the ministers' assurances to rule in favour of narrow interpretations. But all the incentives and imperatives of bureaucratic government push towards widening the scope of and adding functions to the system. Rigorous Parliamentary oversight will be constantly necessary to prevent function creep.

There will be inaccuracies on the register and failures to manage it correctly. Only 2% of the British public believe the data will be totally accurate; the majority opinion varies between 41% who think it will be largely accurate, and 48% who think there will be a good or great deal of inaccurate information on it.

Confidentiality will be a major concern, with 66% not trusting the government to avoid divulging information improperly, and a whopping 82% thinking that there is at least some danger that individual civil servants will breach confidentiality.[59] As it is, the Act states that only certain public bodies – the Security Service, Secret Intelligence Service, GCHQ, the Serious Organised Crime Agency, the police, Revenue and Customs, a government department including government departments of Northern Ireland, and authorities which administer other documents that can be used for identification – can share information on the register without the subject's consent.[60] This list might give some cause to worry, especially after recent spying scandals involving paramilitary forces in Northern Ireland. On top of these, it is reckoned that 265 government departments and 44,000 private sector organisations will be accredited to use it.[61]

The size and scope of the register is immense. Someone registered at birth would have to remain on it for possibly upwards of 100 years, or, put another way, nearly twice the history of computing (records would be upgraded every ten years). The effort, and scope for error, of upgrading to new systems would be huge. The number of errors, if there were (say) 100 million entries in the register, would be colossal, even if the percentage was very small. The Home Office itself estimates that there would be at least 163 million identity verification transactions annually,[62] but this is surely a massive underestimate.

Note also that the identification key would be used by many government departments in their own databases; each department will store information generated in their own interactions with people. It will make absolute sense to use ID card numbers as an indexing system for that information, but that means that amalgamating databases across departments will be trivially simple – all that the departments in question need do is line up the ID card number. Furthermore, the aim of reducing identity theft doesn't seem any nearer, despite that supposedly being one of the register's aims.[63] The current system of a loosely-coordinated cluster of identities associated with a person is not terribly secure, but the ID card is an all-eggs-in-one-basket approach. Creating one über-identity means that not only will the government have created a one-stop shop for identity thieves, but also the potential effects of theft are magnified by so much more.

3

COMPUTER SECURITY MEETS HUMAN IDIOCY: PRIVACY ENHANCING TECHNOLOGIES AND THEIR LIMITS

The candlestick that the Rev Green brains his victims with in the library is not just a weapon; it started life as a useful household tool. Similarly with computer technology – it can be used for good or evil. We should not assume that privacy is passively under threat from technology. In many cases the main *response* to a threat to privacy is technological. Privacy-Enhancing Technologies (PETs) cannot be the whole solution to the privacy problem – legislation, commercial incentives and international agreements will also come into the mix[64] – but they are important nonetheless.

Operating systems

The first line of defence for the ordinary user of computers is the operating system (OS), the program that manages all the hardware and software resources of the computer, and provides the interface to the human user. The most common operating systems are versions of Microsoft's Windows, including Windows 2000, Windows XP and Windows Vista; Windows is used on upwards of 90% of the world's one billion PCs. Other OSs include the MacOS, which is used on Apple Macintosh computers, and Linux, which has been developed using 'open source' methods, meaning that it is not treated as a piece of intellectual property, but rather is developed collaboratively by independent developers working in common as volunteers.

One common tactic for hackers is to try to seize control of some parts of the computer by dropping little pieces of software called 'malware' (including viruses and worms) onto the system; these might attempt to run particular programs using your computer, or alternatively gather information about you. The OS of the computer is very important here, as (a) the malware has to entice it to let it sit on the computer's hard disc, and (b) it will have to run the malware. Security is therefore an extremely important secondary function of the OS.

Microsoft is here at a disadvantage, as it has a virtual monopoly of the OS market. In the first place, Microsoft was relatively slow to wake up to the security risks, and so earlier versions of Windows were not as secure as they could have been. The latest version, Windows Vista, was written from scratch to try to ensure greater security; however, this turned out to be a very large task even for the workforce of 8,000 employed on it, and some of the more ambitious security features had to be abandoned.[65] Secondly, its monopoly makes Windows the main target of hackers, so it is inherently less secure thanks, ironically, to its dominance. And thirdly, viruses and worms that affect Windows spread very quickly, because there are so many other machines running Windows that they can spread to. A worm that throve on Linux, say, would have fewer machines to attack; even if it compromised a machine and spread itself via an email address book, by the law of averages most of the people in the address book would be running Windows, not Linux, and so the worm would be quite likely to die out naturally.

Operating systems are now so large and complex that security holes are inevitable; it is impossible to anticipate all possible forms of attack. Discovery of a flaw in an OS is usually followed by a period of intense research in working out how to stop it, and then the company issues an upgrade, called a *patch*, which is a piece of software added to the OS to deal with that particular flaw. Most machines' operating systems keep in constant contact with their developers, and can be configured to update automatically with new patches when they become necessary.

CRYPTOGRAPHY

One of the most important computational methods for ensuring privacy is cryptography, the deliberate jumbling of messages to prevent them being read by snoopers. Of course, one wants the message to be readable by the intended recipient, so the jumbling has to be reversible, and there must be a guaranteed way of unjumbling it. If the jumbling is very simple, then an interloper will be able to break the code, but if it is very complex, then though more secure it might be more trouble to decode the message than it is worth. One typical jumbling and unjumbling, or more properly, encryption and decryption method is to use a mechanical method or algorithm (called a cipher), with an important extra parameter called a key. Once the message is encrypted, it cannot be decrypted without knowing the method *and* being in possession of the key.

Let's consider a very simple example. A common code, known to all school-children, is to shift letters along the alphabet, so A might be written as B, B as C and so on up to Z which goes back to A. The shift can be any number of letters along – if it is five letters along, then A becomes F, B becomes G and so on, up to Z which goes back to E. So with this trivial code, the key is the number of letters the message is shifted along, a number between 0 and 25 (0 would leave the message unchanged). So if the key is 17, the message MEET ME AT THREE becomes DVVK DV RK KYIVV.

This, of course, is a highly inadequate code; the relative frequency of the letters remains the same, and so (as readers of the Sherlock Holmes story about the dancing men will know) if you have enough message you can make a guess at the key. E is the most common letter in the English language, so we might assume V stood for E. T is the next most common letter, so we might assume that K stood for T. That assumption gives us most of our message – *EET *E *T T**EE – while also suggesting the hypothesis that the key is 17. Completing cracking the code is then trivial.

A slightly more complicated cipher would shift each letter differently. Suppose our key is a well-known word such as PREVENTION. The method might then work by turning the key into a series of numbers based on each letter. So $P = 16$, $R = 18$ and so on; the key becomes 16–18–5–22–5–14–20–9–15–14. Now the message is encrypted by shifting the first letter along 16 positions in the alphabet, the second 18, the third 5 and so on. Once we reach the end we start back at 16 again. So now MEET ME AT THREE becomes CWJP RS UC IVHWJ. With this more complex method we get a trickier encryption. In the simple method, each letter is encoded in the same way, but in this more complex method, the Es are encoded as respectively W, J, S, W and J. However, there is still a bit of repetition, because the double E in MEET is encoded using the letters R and E of the key PREVENTION. Because the key is shorter than the message, we have to go back to the start of the key, which means that the double E in THREE is also encoded using the R and E, so both pairs are encoded as WJ. Given enough data, this variant would also be crackable by a spy prepared to spend the time and trouble.

Obviously cryptography gets a *soupçon* more sophisticated than this. For instance, the Data Encryption Standard (DES) was an important cipher adopted as a standard by the US government in the 1970s. DES takes a piece of text and encrypts it by doing a series of operations on blocks of 64 characters (or bits), with a key of length 56 bits. The method is deeply complicated, but even so DES can be cracked by a brute force attack (i.e. trying every possible key in turn) in a relatively short space of time (hours rather than days). The Advanced Encryption Standard (AES) was designated the DES's successor in 2001, and using a key of 256 bits is much more secure. Nevertheless, DES remains in use in a number of common applications including cashpoint machines and email systems; despite its not being very secure, no-one has ever proved that they have lost money as a result of a criminal cracking a DES code.

DES and AES are examples of so-called symmetric key algorithms, where both the sender and receiver of the message use the same key. These are relatively insecure in that two people need to have the key, and therefore there are two access points to the key for an enemy. The key has to be communicated from the originator to the other user, in which case it might be intercepted on its journey. And if the encryption system is intended to serve a community of users, we have an immediate dilemma. Should there be one key for the whole community, in which case it is correspondingly easier for a spy to get hold of, or a different key for each pair in the community, which gets very complicated to manage especially when the community is large and messages have to be broadcast to several people at a time? So a method of using 'asymmetric' keys, so-called 'public key cryptography', was developed where the encoded message has two keys, one public and one private.[66]

The two keys are mathematically-related, but in such a way that the private key cannot easily be derived from the public key. As its name suggests, the public key is publicly-known, and is used for encrypting the message; the private key is not distributed publicly, and is used for decryption. Without the private key, the message cannot be decrypted and read. So if I want to send you a message, I look up your public key and encrypt the message with that. Now it can only be decrypted by your private key, so it doesn't matter if the message is intercepted, even by someone who knows your public key. As long as you don't reveal your private key, the message can't be cracked. Public key cryptography was invented at Britain's super-secret Government Communications Headquarters (GCHQ), although, perhaps appropriately, they kept the invention a secret, which meant that the credit went to researchers who discovered the principle independently. One of the most important public key algorithms is RSA, named after its three inventors Ron Rivest, Adi Shamir and Leonard Adleman, which is used in many e-commerce applications; if the keys are long enough, the code is still too complex to break.

The process for creating public and private keys is much more complicated than the keys we were using earlier. For example, the

Diffie-Hellman key exchange protocol demands some tricky maths and is very hard to crack.[67] Suppose April and May want to agree on a numerical key for a code. They begin by agreeing on a prime number (let us say 17), and a number called a base, usually 2 or 5 – let us say 5. Each now has to choose a number and keep it secret – suppose April chooses 9 and May chooses 13. Then it gets complicated.

April first sends May the result of a calculation – the remainder of the base to the power of her secret integer when it is divided by the prime number. So she raises 5 to the power 9 (1,953,125), divides it by 17 and takes the remainder, which is 12. So April sends a 12 to May.

May also needs to get out her maths book, and do the same calculation with her secret number: 5 to the power 13 (1,220,703,125), and get the remainder when she divides it by 17, i.e. 3, which she sends to April.

Now it is April's turn with the calculator. She takes the number May has sent her (3), raises it to the power of her own secret number ($3^9 = 19,683$) and finds the remainder when she divides it by 17, which is 14.

May does the same, taking the number April sent her (12), raises it to the power of her secret number ($12^{13} = 106,993,205,379,072$) and finds the remainder when she divides it by 17, which is – hey! – 14.

So by doing a little bit of tortuous arithmetic, April and May each arrive at the key secretly. All their communications can be in public. The base (5), the prime number (17), and the results of their calculations (12 and 3) can be sent without fear of them being intercepted, because they cannot be used on their own to find the key (14). April has a secret integer (9) which she doesn't send to anyone, and she uses that to compute the key, which again she doesn't send to anyone, and the same for May. Of course, this is a small example, and it wouldn't be too hard to crack – after all the key must be less than the prime number, which in this case is 17, and cannot be 0, so there are only 16 possibilities. But if the prime number and the secret integers were chosen as very large numbers indeed (hundreds of digits long), then there would be no efficient way of finding the secret integers mathematically.

That is certainly a clever way of doing things, but it is still vulnerable to attack – a so-called 'man in the middle' attack, whereby a would-be eavesdropper June pretends to April that she is May, and pretends to May that she is April, and thereby can receive some information about their arrangements. This suggests the desirability of being able to authenticate communications, and fortunately public key methods can help here too.

The asymmetric key idea suggests the notion of 'digital signatures'. The insight here is that someone who has created a piece of information or a digital document may wish to make it clear to a reader that the document was written by that person. If it was a paper document, she might sign it, or she might seal it with sealing wax and press her signet ring to create an impression in the wax. Signatures and seals can be forged, but generally speaking they are decent methods of ensuring authenticity – we use them all the time even today. The point about a signature is that it is easy for the correct person to create, and hard for another to forge, and a digital signature is a digital version of the same thing. Some extra information in a particular form is added to a digital document, which can be checked to ensure that the information is in the right form. The trick is to ensure that the signature is easy for the signer to produce and hard for others to forge.

A digital signature system is made up of three ciphers. The first produces a pair of keys for the signer. One is the public key, which can be distributed and which is used to verify the signature, while the other is the private key used for the signing. The second cipher takes a message and the private key, and uses that to create a signature. The third is the verification algorithm that takes the public key, the message and the signature, and gives a thumbs up for a verified signature, and a thumbs down for a forgery.

Digital signatures are extremely useful for authenticating messages. They can be used to make sure that a message comes from the correct source, or to ensure the integrity of a message – if a message has been altered in any way, so will the signature be, and the tampering can thereby be detected. So, for instance, if April and May digitally sign their communications as well as sending each other the results of their calculations, they can avoid the man in the middle attack on their security.

Public key and digital signature systems do have drawbacks, unfortunately. In particular, they only work if the public key is properly associated with the right people. In the example of April, May and June, the whole system only works if we know that communications purporting to come from April and May actually do. June's man in the middle attack stops the system working correctly, because neither April nor May could be sure that messages purporting to come from the other were genuine.

To work properly, a public key system demands an extra layer of support, which is called a public key infrastructure (PKI), to communicate the public keys and associate them with the right people using digital certificates. So, for instance, a Secure Electronic Transactions certificate (SET), which allows credit card transactions over the Internet, links a consumer with (i) an identity, (ii) the right to authorise a charge against a Visa account, and (iii) the public key to verify a payment authorisation. The SET certificate, in effect, acts as a digital version of one's Visa card.[68]

The PKI acts as a guarantor of the public key. April encrypts some information, and signs the document using her private key. May receives the encoded message, and applies to the certification authority within the PKI for April's digital certification, which she can then use to extract the public key and decrypt the message.

But we must beware of talking as if the technology can solve all problems alone. PKIs are only as good as the human administrative systems that support them. The PKI could administer the certificates themselves perfectly, with totally secure computers and communications, but it must also interact with the real world. For instance, it is essential that the identity used in the certificate really does belong to the person it represents, and that can only be established via some administration system creating and maintaining a database securely. The fiddling about with certificates and encoding and decoding can become very tedious and user-unfriendly. And if someone loses their private key, then all the messages are lost – even if they keep receiving messages encoded with the public key, they can't read them because the private key is needed to decrypt them. The problem with the online world is that it is getting larger and larger, and so security really needs to be scalable; a system that is usable in a small environment (such as a company IT department, where everyone knows everyone else) may not work so well where there are orders of magnitude more strangers interacting in various different ways and using lots of separate systems. PKI is a good solution, but it may well not be a practical solution to the privacy problem in a real business environment, or for inexperienced users.[69]

Another alternative way of using asymmetric keys to preserve privacy is to develop a so-called 'web of trust', where the centralised PKI is avoided. In a web of trust, everyone trusts someone, although over the entire network of people no-one will know, still less trust, everyone. But there is enough trust in the network to hold it together. The best-known example of the web of trust approach is called Pretty Good Privacy (PGP),[70] although later versions of PGP can work with centralised authorities as well.

PGP is basically an asymmetric public key system, so it has the usual requirement to bind the public key to the sender of a message. Eschewing the complexities of the centralised PKI that make it hard to scale up, the PGP system envisages a third person digitally signing a certificate that connects the public key with the sender of the message. The basic requirement of that transaction is that the receiver of the message trusts the third party to be reliable and to act in good faith. You needn't trust the sender of the message, and the sender need neither trust you, nor the third party. So whenever April needs to send a message to May with a secure certificate saying that the message really does come from April, then all they have to do is to agree on a third person whom May trusts to certificate the message. Over time, a reasonably-sized network of trusted introducers can be built up, which will be enough to keep the whole system going. Such endorsements are strongly dependent on offline relationships, and will vary according to context. An endorsement by one person will be taken as valid in some online communities, and not in others, and clearly the more business you do, the more business you will be enabled to do.[71]

Such networks do avoid at least some of the difficulties of a centralised PKI system, but have drawbacks of their own. Any kind of reputation-based system such as a web of trust is hard for new users to break into. If you have had lots of dealings with people in the system, then you will be able to find endorsers through your web, but a neophyte who has not made any transactions yet will find it much harder. On the other hand, if it is easy for a new user to work his way into a system, then it will be easy for potential adversaries to get in there too – all such an adversary has to do is to take part in a number of straightforward, honest transactions in order to build a reputation, and then use that reputation for evil ends. Any system that is good at keeping adversaries out will be harder to break into for honest people. And ultimately, a web of trust spreads responsibility across various endorsers – it is not clear who you would sue in the event of being harmed by fraud. At least with a PKI system you can sue the central authority who let you down.

THE WOOD FOR THE TREES: STEGANOGRAPHY

Another way of being private is to hide somewhere no one would think to look – or afford the time to look. Steganographic techniques seek to hide the information one wants to remain private in places that others would not think to look, or else have insufficient time to monitor and analyse. For instance, one can hide messages in the bit patterns of digital images or music. A whole set of resources and techniques for doing this are available on the Web: the Steganography Analysis and Research Center identifies 625 digital techniques – and offers counter measures.[72]

The trick with steganography is to make encoding difficult to detect. To do this one needs to ensure that the changes to the 'carrier' (i.e. the background) due to the injection of the 'payload' (i.e. the interesting message) are visually and statistically negligible. The size of representations in digital media make this eminently possible. If we take an average colour digital image, each pixel will be represented by 24 bits of information. The red, green and blue components of the image each have 8 of the 24 bits of colour depth. Take three pixels and one could encode an ASCII letter on one bit each of a red, a green and a blue component. Messages can be embedded in such ways very easily. And to make it harder the images can also be compressed and modified in other ways that hide the fact that a payload is there at all. This is recognised by Governments – a US Document published in 2006 states that because 'steganography secretly embeds additional, and nearly undetectable, information content in digital products, the potential for covert dissemination of malicious software, mobile code, or information is great.'[73]

It appears all too likely that those who want to remain private for the worst of reasons see the opportunities. The al-Fajr Information Center, a jihadi organization, publishes *Technical Mujahid*, a magazine released once every two months that is available online. A training article from February 2007 outlines steganography; the author appears to be an expert on the subject judging from the details included such as image pixels, mathematical equations to prevent distortions in pictures used to hide data and the disadvantages of encryption software available on the market. Once again the technological arms race is one in which smart methods of remaining hidden are co-evolving with smart ways of detecting the presence of an object of interest.

Identification and Authentication

Cryptography protects privacy by making information impossible for others to read, while steganography hides it, but preventing others from understanding information is not the only type of privacy. In the offline world, we keep our own space private with fences, walls and locks, and to protect our online spaces we have more or less the same approach – except that the security barriers are passwords, access control lists and firewalls.

A password is a sequence of characters that is usually remembered by heart, although it is best not to use a memorable one. The more random the password, the better it is – b4D3kk2Uo is much better than Dinah (especially if Dinah is one's cat). If one uses 26 capital letters, 26 lower case letters and 10 digits, that creates a set of 62 available characters, and there will be 13,537,086,546,263,552 possible 9-character passwords; on the other hand, there are 23,762,752 5-letter names, even if we give ourselves the option of beginning with either a capital or a lower case letter. This illustrates an important point, that if it is known that a password has some internal structure to help it to be memorable, it is easier to crack. If a mechanised attempt to crack a password uses a dictionary of English words, it will do better, all things being unequal, than a random generator if people tend to use real words. A password system is always vulnerable to brute force attack (i.e. trying out every possible password in turn), because a computer will be able to generate the complete list in a short amount of time. So most systems only allow a small maximum number of attempts.

A firewall stands between an online space and less trusted areas. Whenever a communication comes from a less trusted source, the firewall stops it and alerts the owner of the space, who can then decide whether or not to allow it through. Like many types of online security system, a firewall is governed by a policy, which is set up to rule out certain types of communication and allow others. Different types of firewall protect against different types of threat – are you worried primarily about getting a computer virus (in which case you will be looking out for suspicious emails), or do you have sensitive information that you wish to protect (in which case you will be looking out for any attempt to access your computer remotely)?

All these methods are intended to allow the identification and authentication of potential entrants into your online space. During identification, the entrant tells you who he is, and you can choose (or not) to believe him. Online, an identification method should associate the person's message with a representation of an identity. But to be secure, one should not simply take that assertion of identity at face value; one needs to authenticate it, by taking some investigative step to ensure that the correct identity is being asserted. In the offline world we show photographs, or produce signatures, and similar steps need to be taken online, including digital signatures.

The standard method of identification and authentication is a username and password – this works pretty well, but ultimately is not strong enough to keep a determined adversary out, hence the development of alternatives. In general, there are three methods for authenticating identities: the person can produce (a) something they own, (b) something they know, or (c) something that is irrevocably part of them.[74] An owned item might be a key, or a signet ring, or in the digital world it might be a smart card. A known item is usually a password, or the answer to a personal question ('What is your mother's maiden name?'). The final method involves some kind of personal characteristic, perhaps most likely a biometric, which we discuss below. Quite often, complex authentication systems involve a combination of these, such as a smart card activated by a password (the most common example of this is a bank card which also needs a PIN to gain access to one's account).

A very important question is who stores all the information that allows authentication to take place; if they are not trusted, the system will not work. In 2001, Microsoft launched a system called Passport that held identifying information, including credit card numbers, and acted as an identification service verifying users' ID by passing information to accredited websites. All the information was held in a central database, which put Microsoft in the position of holding, and having to protect, every user's identifying data. This was not a success. Microsoft's latest identity management system, CardSpace, avoids this central database; personal information is held by trusted third parties such as banks and credit card companies (who hold the information anyway). The system, by doing away with passwords (which people tend to manage rather badly) aims to allow humble users access to secure cryptographic protocols which are normally reserved for governments and big corporations.[75]

You don't get something for nothing. The stronger the security, the harder the system is to use, and the more expensive it is to administer. So the security method should be closely correlated with the risks involved; a powerful system with cryptography, secret keys, one-time passwords (a password used once and then discarded), or complex and intrusive biometrics would be worth it only if the potential loss through unauthorised access was large. If the risk was relatively small, then simple passwords would do. And if one wants to attract lots of users (as, for example, an e-commerce site would), then simplicity is a definite plus – if your customers always had to go through a complex and hard-to-remember ritual of identification and authentication every time they shopped with you, you wouldn't have any customers. Security is expensive, and context determines how complex it should be.[76]

Biometrics

Much of the growth of the technologies we are talking about has come about through "the disappearance of the body". The root of an identification is often a connection between two pieces of data, such as a bank account and a signature.

However, whenever an identification is grounded in data, there is always the possibility that fake data may have been substituted into the transaction (e.g. a forged signature). This has led to the desire for, and development of, *biometrics*, the measurement of biological data. The idea is to find some characteristic of a person that is unique to them, and either unchangeable or likely to remain stable over an extended period of time, and then to use a measurement of that characteristic as a basis for identification.

In a typical scenario, the subject gives a number of samples of the biometric, which are then digitised and stored on a database. The biometric could then be used either to identify the subject out of a group (a match against several records), or authenticate identity (a match against a single record). Obviously matching against a group is more complex, and error-prone. The biometric has to be unique, which in practice means that it is measured in such a way as to render the probability of someone else having the same measurement acceptably small. If the demands of the test are very harsh, then it is possible that the subject will be incorrectly rejected (and a stringent test will also add to the cost of using the biometric); on the other hand, if the test is relatively weak, then the danger is that an impostor will be incorrectly accepted.

One biometric much-loved in detective fiction is the human smell, with the sensitive 'readers' being dogs, particularly blood-hounds. The sample is an item of clothing which is linked to the individual whose movements are to be traced, and then the 'reader' is able to follow traces of the biometric odour through a complex environment to discover the present location of the sub-ject. This biometric has the advantage that the 'readers' are mobile and possess basic intelligence (canine neural nets) which allows them to steer through unpredictable terrain.

There are a number of biometrics either in use, or in the stages of advanced research. The most obvious is face recogni-tion, which has been used ever since photography has made pos-sible accurate and objective representation of the human face. We are shown a picture of the subject, and invited to compare the face on offer with the photograph; this kind of non-automated check is the basis for most passport or ID card checks even now. It is a cheap method, and because humans have evolved extremely good face recognition abilities, reasonably accurate, although it may be spoofed by disguises of various kinds.

However, face recognition can also be done automatically. The study of faces has long been a research topic in artificial intelligence, and the better systems have obvious applications in information security. Such systems work by establishing a number of measurements of what are called nodal points, such as the distance between the eyes, the width of the nose and so on. A typical system will rely on twenty or so such points. The face needs to be represented – for instance on a video or still photograph image – but any worthwhile system will also need to understand faces that are turned away, different expressions, lighting conditions, spectacles, facial hair etc.

The accuracy of face recognition is not as high as other biometrics, so one would not necessarily want to use it to secure one's own privacy. Indeed, face recognition is less likely to be used to secure privacy for the individual, as for the purposes of surveillance of individuals by an observer – in other words to *invade* privacy rather than protect it. Face recognition is a particularly good system for surveillance, as it does not require the subject's co-operation to be useful (unlike, say, iris scanning). Automatic systems have been deployed in several places, perhaps most famously by the London Borough of Newham in its CCTV system, although apparently it hasn't succeeded in spotting many villains.[77]

Another very common and well-known biometric is the fingerprint. Again, traditionally a law enforcement tool, it is now beginning to become part of the armoury of methods for securing privacy, as many types of computer now boast fingerprint readers to allow secure logins. Whereas face recognition is the most common manual identification technique, fingerprinting takes up about two thirds of the overall market for automatic biometrics.[78] Other less prominent methods, all growing in popularity, include iris scanning, retinal scanning, voice recognition and gait recognition (using the way someone walks to recognise them).

There is no perfect biometric – much depends on what you want it to do. Common requirements for a biometric include *universality* (each person should have it), *uniqueness* (no two people should have the same measurements), *permanence* (it should neither change nor be alterable), *collectability* (it should be measurable quantitatively), *performance* (it should be measurable efficiently, accurately, quickly, robustly and cheaply), *acceptability* (the measurement process needs to be acceptable to the public, so for example, should not involve surgery or other dangerous procedures; indeed, in societies where veiling is practised, even face recognition may not be acceptable) and *non-circumvention* (the system should not be easy to fool).[79]

Biometrics have one huge advantage over other ways of establishing an identity for a person, and that is that they are strongly bound to the subject; in many cases change will result in pain or physical harm. This makes the bond between the digital presence and the person very strong. But for the same reason, many people regard biometrics as potential *threats* to privacy. Tracking or surveillance using biometrics requires that the tracker has some access to the original biometric template. If the biometric is designed primarily to *secure* privacy for the individual, for instance by allowing a restricted number of people access to something, then there is no need to store the template in a public place; it could be stored on a person's smart card (say), which could then be used to gain access. Without the smart card, the biometric could not be used. To gain access, the person would need to be in possession of the smart card *and* have a biometric corresponding closely enough to the template on the card. Hence losing the card would be an inconvenience, but it would not allow a breach of privacy.

Much of the explosion in growth of biometrics since 2005 or so has been in the commercial sector; once more it is convenience (and small incentives from retailers, bankers and others) that have persuaded people to adopt or accept technologies even at the risk of encroaching on privacy. In the USA, three million people regularly pay for goods at supermarkets by scanning fingerprints and using a PIN. Two million Japanese have adopted a system whereby their palms are scanned to withdraw cash from a cashpoint. Dutch bank ABN-AMRO is about to unveil a telephone banking system that will use voice identification to verify customers' identities. The improvement in the accuracy of biometrics has driven this growth, for two reasons. First, they have become commercially viable as well as a tool for governments. In particular, the risk of false positives (in this case, that a fraudster could fake your biometric) is reduced because many commercial transactions are face to face between customer and checkout operator, and someone making repeated payment attempts would quickly attract attention. And second, they have become more inclusive. It used to be the case that large numbers of people could not be verified by biometrics because of particular problems in the real environment – old people, or people whose hands had been hardened by years of manual labour, or people with eye conditions were often not recognisable by biometrics systems, and therefore missed out on the benefits as well as the surveillance. This is less of a problem nowadays.[80]

Biometrics are also beginning to migrate onto the Internet. Of course it would be hard to scan irises or fingerprints online in real time without fitting computers with dedicated scanners, but behavioural biometrics do have the potential to open up the Internet. It looks as if it may be possible to identify people by the way in which they type a password, or by voice recognition over the microphones that are now routinely built into laptops.[81]

THE HUMAN IN THE LOOP

So we might worry about the technology being intrusive, but there are many technologies that can help secure privacy as well as eroding it. However, we always have to remember that technology is a tool, not a solution. It is used by people, who may be more fallible than the systems they deploy. They might use the system wrongly, or use it correctly to do the wrong thing. And it may be set up incorrectly.

In the case of identification – particularly biometrics – a key moment is the initialisation of the system. The biometric template is established on a database or card as the identifying factor for a person. But as Fred Piper and colleagues point out, there is only one stage of a person's life at which we can have total confidence in the claim to identity: when the umbilical cord still attaches that person to his or her mother, and even then our confidence is only as strong as our confidence in the identification of the mother.[82] At any subsequent stage, it is possible that another person has substituted for the person to be identified, and that the biometric attachment is therefore to the impostor. And even a properly-verified biometric can still be undermined. One identification option often mentioned is to implant microchips into people to store and broadcast identity, but we cannot rule out the possibility that the chip could be surgically removed and replaced, or that the information could be changed via remote access. Even if we take a DNA sample from a baby when it is still attached to its mother, there is still the possibility of substituting another sample on its journey to the lab for analysis. There is no absolutely foolproof method of securing the identity of a person, even via the most accurate of biometrics.

This leads us to the general question of administering technological systems to enhance privacy – the technologies may be ever so perfect, but they need to be used properly. All our assumptions about the way a privacy-enhancing technology works are premised on the administration being done correctly and the infrastructure being trustworthy. Technical issues are often discussed. Does the machine work correctly, and how can we spot a fault? Could someone hack into the system or sabotage it? But in practice the more serious issue is whether the system works with the people, resources and incentives currently in place.

One important aspect is the user. Even if the system is designed to protect privacy, and even if we assume the user has every incentive to learn the system and use it correctly, that will not stop elementary errors being made, perhaps due to unfamiliarity with the system, perhaps because all the ramifications of it are not understood. And why should they be? If PETs are to become a ubiquitous feature of life then surely they should be operable by the least educated, the least numerate, and those most bored or repelled by computers. Luddites have rights too.

And how are users supposed to be sure that their preferences are exactly modelled by the behavioural parameters of the system they are using? For instance, they may have ideas about what communications they will trust from the outside world. They may be using a firewall with a privacy policy. But few people will be able to verify for themselves that the privacy policy implements their preferences. And presented with a question (for instance, if a security certificate is refused on a secure site that they are visiting), can they always be sure that they will be able to choose the option from the list that best corresponds to their preferences?

Of course they can't. The human in the loop is a weakness of any privacy system – but that does not mean that all we have to do is to engineer the human out of the loop, for the simple reason that the human is the basis of the loop in the first place. The loop is to protect the human. And so any system has to be tolerant of misuse and failure.

The level of failure can be quite extraordinary. In a remarkable piece of evidence to the US Senate Committee on Governmental Affairs, Kevin Mitnick, once dubbed 'the world's most wanted cybercriminal' gave a fascinating picture.

The most complex element in information security is the people who use the systems in which the information resides. Weaknesses in personnel security negate the effort and cost of … physical, network and computer system security.

Social engineering, or "gagging", is defined as gaining intelligence through deception. Employees are trained to be helpful, and to do what they are told in the workplace. The skilled social engineer will use these traits to his or her advantage as they seek to gain information that will enable them to achieve their objectives… In my successful efforts to social engineer my way into Motorola [an American electronics firm], I used a three-level social engineering attack to bypass the information security measures then in use. First I was able to convince Motorola Operations employees to provide me, on repeated occasions, the pass code on their security access device, as well as the static PIN. The reason this was so extraordinary is that the pass code on their access device changed every 60 seconds: every time I wanted to gain unauthorized access, I had to call the Operations Center and ask for the password in effect for that minute.

The second level involved convincing the employees to enable an account for my use on one of their machines, and the third level involved convincing one of the engineers who was already entitled to access one of the computers to give me his password. I overcame that engineer's vigorous reluctance to provide the password by convincing him that I was a Motorola employee, and that I was looking at a form that documented the password that he used to access his personal workstation on Motorola's network – despite the fact that he never filled out any such form! Once I gained access to that machine, I obtained Telnet access to the target machine, access to which I had sought all along.[83]

Similarly, a prosecution in the United Kingdom by the Information Commissioner of a couple for illegally obtaining and selling personal information had absolutely nothing to do with their techie prowess in hacking through firewalls and secure socket layers. Rather,

The couple used 'blagging' techniques to obtain personal information about individuals from a number of organisations including Her Majesty's Revenue and Customs, British Telecom and banks. On a number of occasions the 'blaggers' purported to be employees of these organisations and deceived the true members of staff into disclosing personal information about individuals.

The evidence gathered by the ICO showed that the couple had obtained account details, income tax information and ex-directory telephone numbers relating to a number of different 'victims'.[84]

Indeed, one of the first major crises for Gordon Brown's new UK government happened in November 2007, literally as we were correcting the proofs for this book, when the personal records of 25 million people (nearly half the UK population), including sensitive details such as National Insurance and bank account numbers, were lost in the post. Computer discs with the details of the 7.25 million families claiming child benefit were couriered (against the rules) from HM Revenue and Customs to the National Audit Office. The discs were not sent by recorded delivery, and they went missing. The information was not encrypted, though the discs were passport protected. At the time of writing, although the head of Revenue and Customs had resigned, the full extent of the political fallout was not yet clear. Whether or not more heads roll, the point we have to note is that the system contained a large number of security measures, which were collectively adequate to prevent this disaster. But nothing about a rule can ensure that it is followed; in this case, it appears that a junior official put the discs in the internal mail system without following proper procedures. You cannot legislate for such inexperience or lapses of judgement.

Clearly the *system* is the unit of analysis, not the technology. We need to focus on the nexus of people and technologies. We need top-notch technologies, but we also need to use them correctly. Computers won't do it all for us.

CASE STUDY: THEORIES OF PRIVACY MANAGEMENT

It is usually an error to assume that breaches of privacy happen because of evil intent. In the offline world, privacy is generally breached accidentally or unwittingly, and the same is true online – with the added difficulty that sometimes there are no guidelines or methods for stating one's preferences. If I don't know that a piece of information is confidential, I will not take any particular measures to keep it so. We need to be given the tools and language for ensuring that information about us is treated properly.

There is a legal background to such thoughts. Warren and Brandeis' 'right to be let alone' has morphed into the right to control access to public understanding of oneself. For example, in 1980, the Organisation of Economic Co-operation and Development (OECD) released an influential set of guidelines[85] for a common understanding of privacy across its membership of developed nations. The OECD was concerned that divergent privacy laws across these states would hinder the cross-border flow of information, and so it created the guidelines as a means of setting out basic principles of privacy regulation and requirements. They have proved extremely influential, underpinning most cross-border agreements and national laws. But their scope is generally restricted to demanding limits to the collection of personal data – such data should be relevant to some stated purpose, collected legally, stored securely, and only used in the anticipated context.

Given such limits, it is vital to make it possible for people to say what privacy policies they wish to pursue when they create some digital information. Note that this is a corollary of a tacit assumption that privacy is a subjective requirement, need or preference. Different people have different views of what should be private. That means that authorities cannot simply identify information that should be private and insist that all companies keep it so. People must be able to reach their own decisions about what should be private, and what gains they would hope to make by releasing information about themselves.

To give some idea of the sorts of interactions possible here, we will examine a couple of initiatives in this area. An important example of a privacy policy management system is the Platform for Privacy Preferences (P3P)[86] developed by the World Wide Web Consortium (W3C), the main international standard-setting body for the WWW. P3P was developed as a result of the unplanned evolution of e-commerce, where firms were using computing and communications links to gather information about their customers.

Cookies are the standard gizmo used to track customers, they are little pieces of data that are used to tell a website when someone is accessing it. A site places a cookie on the browser used to access it, and the browser returns the cookie whenever it accesses the site again. This means that the site can recognise particular return users. Sometimes used for annoying reasons by a company (e.g. for targeted advertising), cookies have more practical and general value, for instance by allowing shoppers to have persistent virtual shopping baskets (one can log out of an e-commerce site, and log in later with the contents of one's basket still intact). Cookies are not dangerous – they are not special types of programs or viruses – but they do allow others to gather information about one's Internet use. One can ensure one's privacy by setting one's Web browser to refuse cookies, but that can mean that one then cannot access some websites (and one's shopping basket will empty irritatingly every time one logs out).

This is the classic type of privacy problem – there are many tangible benefits to be had by accepting cookies on one's machine, whereas the costs are intangible. There is no way around this dilemma – we either protect our privacy or we enjoy the fruits of e-commerce. We can't do both. But equally, many companies and websites do not particularly want to invade privacy without permission; of course the information so gathered is valuable and it is easy to gather but on the other hand responsible companies do not wish to irritate their customers or behave in so irresponsible a manner that people stop using the Web to do their shopping.

For the consumer it is hard to decide, and also hard to police, if we are constantly having to change the settings on our browsers from accepting cookies to not. So P3P is a sort of language or protocol that allows sites and browsers to undertake more complex conversations with each other about attitudes to privacy. And even better, these conversations take place automatically, without the user having to think too hard about it.

A P3P-compliant website has a privacy policy that states clearly and unambiguously what information it will gather, and what it will do with it. It can use P3P to state:

- Whether it will store information that can identify the user.
- What information exactly will be stored. Will it, for instance, include the email address of the user? The IP address of the machine?

- What the information will be used for. Will it, for example, be used for marketing, or merely to allow the personalisation of the interaction?
- Whether the information will be passed on to any third parties.
- How long the information will be stored.
- Whether the user will have access to the information (for example, to check it is correct).

Consumers will have their own ideas of whether the site's policy is OK from their point of view, and then can choose to interact with it or not. So, for instance, if the user's browser is set up to ensure that information gathered about browsing patterns via a cookie should not be passed on to third parties, but the site explains that it will pass on information about browsing patterns to another organisation, then the browser will refuse to allow the cookie to be placed on it. Or the user may have a more complex requirement, for instance that a home address should not be revealed, unless arranging delivery of a purchase. It is clear that P3P does not 'solve' privacy problems – after all, the company running the website could simply lie. It could state in its privacy policy that it will delete information immediately the interaction ceased, but once the information is gathered it could store it and sell it to others. Nothing about the setup here will prevent such misuse. But P3P does give an avenue for people to express the limits to their willingness to allow their privacy to be compromised, and for websites to explain their privacy policies. As long as everyone acts in good faith, then any interactions will meet everyone's constraints.

P3P has its critics. It is said that it is complex and burdensome, and that it depends on someone noticing that a practice might compromise privacy. Far better, it is argued, to establish independent standards, or even laws, that can be used as a baseline.[87]

There are other methods of trying to agree how to express and negotiate privacy preferences. A philosophical theory called contextual integrity, intended to provide principles to cover the transfer of information,[88] tries to uncover the hidden assumptions about why there is an outcry about one type of information transfer, and none about another. For instance, when one goes to the supermarket, one happily wheels around a trolley with sides made of metal rods that allow everyone to see what one has bought. One stands in the checkout with one's purchases clearly on display. But when shopping online, it would seem like an invasion of privacy if one found out that the retailer was storing the information about what has been bought, and was selling that to marketing firms. This is, at first blush, odd, and contextual integrity theory is intended to work out why such differences occur.

This approach rejects the idea that privacy is a simple dichotomy between public and private, and instead supports the idea that there are many types of information that feature in the norms of a given context, which may change in a different context. So, for example, collecting information about someone's marital status may be appropriate at the beginning of a date, but inappropriate in the context of a job interview. The theory assumes that there are three agents connected with the movement of a piece of information: the sender, the receiver and the person who is the subject of the information, and that these agents occupy different roles (e.g. bank manager, interviewer, interviewee, auditor, student) in each context. It then provides a vocabulary to describe precisely the relevance and importance of these roles (e.g. it is appropriate that a lecturer, but not a fellow student, has automatic access to a student's marks in a particular course).

Quite complex formal propositions about privacy can be expressed using the theory, including (it has been shown) genuine pieces of American privacy-related legislation, and in this respect it goes beyond P3P.[89] However, once again, this is a method of talking about privacy norms, not enforcing them. Indeed, within this framework it is actually impossible to say that an agent has broken a norm, so that for example, Californian privacy legislation requiring people to be informed when information about them has been leaked cannot be described at all.

Systems for privacy management

The complexity of the real world is often the central problem in preserving privacy even when good faith is assumed.[90] Hewlett-Packard's Trusted Systems Laboratory in Bristol, UK, has been developing systems to allow companies and organisations to meet their privacy obligations. Such obligations entail certain duties, and it is essential for a large organisation that duties are recognised when they occur, and that recognition is transformed into action – it is all very well for a computer system to dictate that a certain action should take place, but quite another thing for a person (or another computer) to act upon that command in the real world. Information systems and management need to work together in harmony. HP have been experimenting with systems that carry out such duties, such as retaining data securely, deleting it when appropriate, notifying subjects about the data relevant to them, and meeting obligations and expectations. The privacy preferences are encoded into the information being used; the policy 'sticks' to the information, so we can talk about 'sticky' policies.[91] Such systems must represent these obligations, enforce them and monitor that they have been carried out; but of course such a system's enforcement powers are only capable of being used if the obligation management system is successfully integrated into the wider management of the company. Because of the complexity of the interface between the world (and potentially awkward customers), large organisations and the law, it turns out that three separate systems had to be built and then integrated. The HP solution required:

1. A Privacy Policy Enforcement System, which logs the purposes for which data are collected, checks the purpose for which someone wants access to data, deals with data subjects' consent, and enforces access conditions to data set by managers or data subjects.
2. A Privacy Obligation Management System, which manages the obligations (e.g. to destroy the data, or notify the data subjects) that come with possession of the data. Note that this is a different system from (1) – an organisation will have obligations whether or not data is ever actually accessed.
3. A Policy Compliance Checking System, which checks whether information technology systems (such as (1) and (2) above) are adequate for carrying out specific privacy policies (policies which might be expressed using languages such as P3P or contextual integrity theory).[92]

This system seems very difficult, but we sketch it out here to show that, for an organisation that is even moderately complex, and that holds a large quantity of digital information, it is hard to do the right thing even if it always acts in good faith. So murky is the world of privacy preferences that just working out what the right thing is in a particular context is very difficult. Privacy management systems will be essential tools for tomorrow's managers.

4

THE POWER OF POWER: MOORE'S LAW AND PRACTICAL OBSCURITY

MOORE'S LAW, POWER AND PRIVACY

The image of computing has altered over the last couple of decades. Computers used to be cutting edge, exciting, science fiction tools. Now many perceive them as distinctly boring; for instance, the number of people starting computing courses in higher education in the UK fell by 40% between 2001 and 2006, with comparable falls in the US, Canada and other Western countries.[93] At the same time, computers are now ubiquitous, and have transformed our lives.

There is of course a connection between these two trends. A technology which merely has promise can become the subject of all sorts of speculation, positive and negative. At a time when the most common use of computers was to do difficult or repetitive arithmetic, the idea that our lives might be controlled, our memories replaced, all strife expunged from the world by rational thinking machines was an interesting hypothesis to explore. Now that computers do impinge almost everywhere in the lives of people in developed Western democracies, they are actual rather than potential, and consequently dull in comparison. The cyberpunk vision of various bits of cobbled-together kit randomly strewn throughout society more often than not impeding progress, has taken over.

This is the fate of all technologies. To those of us who remember the original appearance of the interplanetary soap-opera *Star Trek*, the whizzy technology on board the USS Enterprise remains iconic. The doors of the ship opened without anyone touching them! With an interesting 'swish' noise! The crew could talk to each other with little communicators! Incredible! But nowadays, what is more boring than an automatic door, which you can find at your nearest supermarket? And Captain Kirk's exotic communicator jargon was somewhat more fascinating than the banalities that most of us broadcast with our mobiles.

How did computers come to be this prevalent, and this, well, *ordinary*, especially as within living memory there were no electronic computers at all? The phenomenon that underpins this new ubiquity is *Moore's Law*. In 1965, Gordon Moore, the founder of the world's largest supplier of computer chips, Intel, wrote a little article looking ahead to 1975 that predicted that computers would continue to provide considerably more bang for your buck as time went on. His eye was fixed as firmly on economic factors as electronic ones.

> Reduced cost is one of the big attractions of integrated electronics, and the cost advantage continues to increase as the technology evolves toward the production of larger and larger circuit functions on a single semiconductor substrate. For simple circuits, the cost per component is nearly inversely proportional to the number of components, the result of the equivalent piece of semiconductor in the equivalent package

containing more components. But as components are added, decreased yields more than compensate for the increased complexity, tending to raise the cost per component. Thus there is a minimum cost at any given time in the evolution of the technology. At present, it is reached when 50 components are used per circuit. But the minimum is rising rapidly while the entire cost curve is falling …. If we look ahead five years, a plot of costs suggests that the minimum cost per component might be expected in circuits with about 1,000 components per circuit (providing such circuit functions can be produced in moderate quantities.) In 1970, the manufacturing cost per component can be expected to be only a tenth of the present cost.

The complexity for minimum component costs has increased at a rate of roughly a factor of two per year …. Certainly over the short term this rate can be expected to continue, if not to increase. Over the longer term, the rate of increase is a bit more uncertain, although there is no reason to believe it will not remain nearly constant for at least 10 years. That means by 1975, the number of components per integrated circuit for minimum cost will be 65,000.

I believe that such a large circuit can be built on a single wafer.[94]

What Moore was saying was that the number of transistors on an integrated circuit doubles every year, at minimum cost per transistor – in other words, on the assumption that a chip's power is proportional to the number of transistors on it, that viable chips were doubling in power annually at that time. A bit more thinking and a bit more observation showed that the doubling was indeed continuing, but at a slightly slower rate of about every 18 months or two years. Moore wasn't particularly interested in setting targets or making firm predictions. He was trying to make the point that electronics would get very much cheaper very quickly.

But the fascination with Moore's Law, as the idea that computers would double in power every 18 months soon became known, was driven by three factors. The first was that Moore's observation, though it was empirically grounded, wasn't just an observation of past behaviour. It was a view based on a deep knowledge of how chips were constructed, and where the possibilities for cost-cutting were likely to emerge, and so was predictive. Second, to many people's astonishment, Moore's Law actually remained true up to 1975 and well beyond. And third, the Law became like a law of economics, if not a law of nature, because the microelectronics industry began to see Moore's Law as a key indicator of success. If the chips that a firm was manufacturing were *not* twice as powerful as the ones they were producing 18 months ago, they were seen as failures.

In fact, Moore's Law remains true even now over 40 years after its initial tentative formulation, although chips are so small and densely packed that the industry is reaching the stage when quantum effects are beginning to be felt (which will ultimately either call a halt to Moore's Law, or require a complete rethink of the physics of computing). The examples Moore used had tens of transistors on them; one of Intel's latest chips, the Dual-Core Intel Itanium 2 Processor, which uses not one but two central processing 'brains' per chip, has billions.

It is this enormous increase in computing power, by a factor of a billion (Moore's Law actually requires an average increase of over 1% per week), that has driven the growth of the computer as a part of our lives. Imagine a problem that took a computer a second to perform in 1965; that means that a computer of the same quantity of hardware in 2005 could do a thousand such calculations every microsecond. Or in terms of memory, imagine a set of chips that could store the content of this book in 1965. A set the same size nowadays could store the contents of every book in every American academic research library.

That is a phenomenal increase, which allows a number of things to happen. Giant quantities of information can be stored. Incomparably many calculations can be made. The productivity gains that information technology allows are straightforward to garner – if a firm's IT infrastructure is stretched by the demands on it at any time, IT managers need only wait a few months before much more powerful computers will be available for the same cost. But what do such increases actually mean for the problems computers can address?

There have always been worries about powerful computers, but most of them seem to be ill-conceived. One influential, if implausible, line of philosophical thought throughout the 1960s and 70s was that as humans are basically nothing more than sophisticated computers, mechanical computers comparable in sophistication will eventually acquire attributes previously thought to be characteristically human (e.g. emotions, problem-solving skills, a sense of evil). In Arthur C. Clarke's *2001: A Space Odyssey*, the computer HAL is clever enough to realise it is about to be shut down, and potent enough to kill off a large number of people in its attempt to prevent that happening.

This of course didn't happen – humans and computers are very different in all sorts of ways. But the power of computers driven by brute force is problematic, as well as incredibly useful, because they can blast their way through vast quantities of data. Information that was hidden can now be exposed, thanks to the progress made. Very important in all sorts of contexts – but not so good for privacy. Ordinary they may be; harmless they are not, for they threaten an important, if informal, defence of privacy – *practical obscurity*.

The collection of information – in effect, attempting to make permanent the traces that our transactions leave behind – changed society in all sorts of ways. Charles Dickens' great novel *Bleak House* (1852–3) is a fine illustration of the context of the evolution of privacy in the nineteenth century. The story tells of an extended family blighted for a generation by its involvement in a labyrinthine legal case *Jarndyce v Jarndyce*. This involvement in itself undermines the privacy of several of the characters – for instance, the young lead characters need the court's permission to live with their guardian John Jarndyce, and one of them even has to apply for leave to change his career.

In the background lurk more sinister forces. An apparently minor incident sends the monstrous lawyer Tulkinghorn on an investigative trail to discover the reason behind it. Behind the event lie years of concealment and guilt, yet all the information that Tulkinghorn needs to solve the mystery exists somewhere on paper. However, so chaotic are the institutional structures that gathering it together to get the correct picture turns *Bleak House* into a detective story. What preserves the integrity of the characters' intimate space is merely the lack of organisation of that information into a coherently indexed whole. It can only be searched by those with the necessary skills, the lawyers Tulkinghorn and Guppy – and even then only because they both have different reasons to search indefatigably.

This introduces practical obscurity as an important factor in the preservation of privacy. The existence of information is one thing, but if its representation does not permit it to be easily queried, then the extraction of important knowledge is quite another. *Bleak House* remains, a century and a half after its composition, the greatest work about the power of information, and a key illustration of the precariousness of the protection provided by practical obscurity.

BRUTE FORCE

How does Moore's Law undermine practical obscurity? Let us begin with a quintessentially human skill: chess. Chess has always been held up by computer scientists as an important task for two main reasons. First, it is correlated with intelligence in humans, at least in the popular understanding. Brainy people play chess, and the brainier the person, the better player they are. And second, it is a well-structured problem. At any stage, the aim of the two players is clear, and the number of allowable moves is a short, well-defined and tractable list. There are no ambiguities; either a move is in accordance with the rules, in which case it is legal, or it is not, in which case it can't happen. So early pioneers such as Alan Turing thought chess would be a good test case of the intelligence of computers.

Chess is a fiendishly difficult game if you want to be sure of winning. At each stage in the game, there might be, let's say, 20 available moves on average. The number of moves in a game might be, again on average, about 25 for each player, or 50 in total. So, starting at the beginning, there might be 20^{50} potential games that may occur (there are probably many more, but this is a rough calculation). This is a very large number, of the order of magnitude of a 1 followed by 65 0s. If you took one second to consider each of these games, then you wouldn't be very far through the process before the universe ended.

So how do mere humans play chess? We play intelligently. We don't consider really stupid moves, we have strategies, spot good moves and anticipate likely responses. Consider a player who thinks 5 moves ahead (which very clever players can). Again assuming an average of 20 available moves at each stage, that is 20^{10} things to think about (another very large number, 10,240,000,000,000), but not all of them are considered. Virtually all potential scenarios are rejected and only the likely ones, a much smaller set amounting to perhaps a couple of dozen moves, are seriously considered.

When computers were large and clunky, they were not intelligent enough to weed out unlikely moves, nor powerful enough to go through all the possibilities. So they would fail, at least when pitted against humans. But they got better. A chess playing computer program written by Dietrich Prinz in 1951 could solve simple problems to mate in two moves. In 1956, a MANIAC I computer could play chess without bishops on a 6x6 board, taking 12 minutes to search 4 moves deep. In 1958, a computer beat a person at chess for the first time, but the human player had been taught the rules only an hour before the game.

MAC HACK VI entered the Massachusetts Amateur Championship of 1966, the first time a computer had entered a chess tournament, and drew one game and lost four. It did beat its first human player in a tournament the next year, and by the end of 1967 had entered four tournaments, winning three games, drawing three and losing twelve. Ten years later, the best computers were serious players: one beat a grandmaster for the first time, in a blitz game, while another won the Minnesota Open with five victories against a single defeat. The first victory over a grand-master in tournament play was 1988. By the early 1990s, the top players – even world champion Garry Kasparov – were occasion-ally losing to computers. In 1996, Kasparov lost a match under tournament conditions to DEEP BLUE – Kasparov won the encounter as a whole 4–2. DEEP BLUE won a return six-match fixture in 1997. A computer had finally beaten the best chess player in the world. Top end computers are now demonstrably superior to people: the seventh-ranked player in the world, Michael Adams, lost to Hydra 5.5–0.5 over six games in 2005.[95]

One would expect progress, as computer chess programmers became more experienced. But such progress? It is not that chess programs play more intelligently than people. They do not: they still search laboriously through most if not all of the possibilities, thinking very stupidly indeed. So how can such stupidity pay off?

The ignorance is accompanied by brute force. Kasparov cal-culates 10 positions every three minutes. While he was doing that, DEEP BLUE would calculate fifty billion positions even in defeat in 1996, and thanks to Moore's Law computing power has increased 100-fold since then. Note the difference that Kasparov's human intelligence and skill makes: he was five billion times slower than the computer, but still won the series. But ultimately, brute force wins the day.

We should not underestimate the sheer power of brute force. In cryptography, however clever the codes one uses, one always has to anticipate the possibility of a brute force attack, an attempt to discover the key to a code by, in effect, trying all the possible keys to decrypt the message. In general, the expected time it takes a brute force attack to succeed on a cipher is proportional to half the number of keys (on average). So given the 2^{56} keys of the American standard DES code it will take 2^{55} (36,028,797,018,963,968) attempts on average to discover the real one. Any cleverer method than brute force that will take longer is not worth thinking about, so one way of defining 'codebreaking' is the discovery of a method that beats brute force. It may be, for a particular cipher, that a brute force method would simply take too long, in which case it can be viewed as, in effect, unbreakable in the absence of a better method. But the goal is always shifting, as the relentless advance of computing power ensures that brute force gets better and better results.

For instance, when DES was developed, in the 1970s, the 2^{55} expected attempts to break it would have exceeded anyone's computational capabilities. However, in 1998, the Electronic Frontier Foundation, an American privacy and civil liberties advocacy group, cracked DES with a machine sporting the somewhat unfortunate name DEEP CRACK, built with custom hardware, in a mere 56 hours, which prompted DES's replacement with AES a few years later.[96]

Data mining and grids

Moore's Law enables us to get very much more from our computers, specifically – in the privacy context – from the increasingly large quantities of *data* that (also thanks to Moore's Law) we can store. Organisations and bureaucracies are always hungry for information, because the more information, the more we know about the world. However, what we need from an information store is *useful* information, which approximates to *knowledge*.[97]

Information gleaned from the automated checkouts of several thousand supermarkets might be comprehensive, but not useful. What we really need are the inferences that that information supports; for instance, that sales of this brand of beans are declining, or sales of that brand of beer and that brand of chocolates are correlated. When we have these inferences, we have something upon which we can act. What we need to do is extract the weak signals from the noisy data.

Getting usable information out of huge datasets is called *data mining*,[98] a complex amalgam of computer science, statistics and information retrieval. Large quantities of data allow the discovery of very occasional relations or very low probabilities. For instance, one can imagine a drug having harmful, but very rare, side effects, affecting perhaps one person in 10,000. During a clinical trial, it is unlikely that such a side effect would be uncovered, or, if it did show itself, it would look as if it were more prevalent than it actually is (suppose, say, that two people out of a thousand tested developed the effect: the probability of it occurring would appear to be 0.2%, not 0.01% which it actually is). But after the drug has been in use for several years and data about its use gathered, there would be enough examples for the exact size of the small probability to be discovered and explored, and commonalities between those who came down with the rare effects isolated. So ultimately it may be discovered that, say, a particular gene or lifestyle contributes to the side effect, which will help at prescription time. Without the huge effort of crunching numbers in giant stores of data, we would not have discovered the side effect, or how to alleviate it.

Data mining is immensely useful in science, commerce, government, and the maintenance of public health. But equally there is clearly a privacy threat when we can extract patterns from large quantities of information. Without the patterns, individual pieces of information would be near-useless; it is a *pattern* of behaviour that reveals someone as having an affair, or being a member of a political party, or an adherent of a religion or cult. Passing by a church once does not make one a member of that church; being in that vicinity every Sunday might raise more valid suspicions. Mining brings out all that is implicit in the raw data.[99]

Data mining, though, remains a challenge – the proportion of relevant data can be tiny. For instance, suppose the problem was to find incriminating content on someone's hard disc. Let us also suppose that the amount of content is fairly extensive – it might be a terrorist manual of about a megabyte. In 12 point text on single sheets of A4, the manual would be printed out on a pile of paper 1.3 inches high. A gigabyte of data would be 110 feet high. A pile of paper as high as Mount Everest would be 263 gigabytes – about the contents of four laptop computers. Finding the relevant and 'interesting' material remains a very tough problem.

In some areas the amount of data produced by information-gathering is still too much for individual computers to perform comfortably. Furthermore, there is an awful lot of computing power around in the world – most computers sit around either doing nothing, or doing something well within their large capacities, such as running word processing applications and email. One way to exploit this spare capacity is to link computers together, connecting them and allowing them to act as a single computer. This allows large organisations to manage their workflow a little more flexibly by making use of idle time on their computers, but perhaps more importantly, it also allows otherwise independent computers to be yoked together to address a single problem.[100] The computing required to solve the problem is distributed across all the computers in what is called a *grid*; the term 'grid' has a handily dual connotation of an array of parallel connected items, and a source of apparently homogeneous power which may be derived, unbeknownst to the users, from a range of heterogeneous sources (as in the electricity grid).

The most famous project to attempt to use the idle resources of other computers is SETI@home, which users download as a screensaver. Whenever the computer's screensaver comes on, SETI begins its work by taking over some of the computer's processing power to sift through signals harvested from space by radio telescopes, looking for regularities which would reveal the presence of intelligent alien life forms (SETI stands for 'Search for Extra-Terrestrial Intelligence').[101] Perhaps unsurprisingly the little green men have remained elusive, but the search goes on. As Moore's Law continues to bite, the amount of computing power available has even enabled the SETI project to improve the resolution of the analysis, allowing the unveiling of 'SETI@home enhanced'.[102] And all this happens in the background, with the volunteers who have subscribed effectively unaware of anything happening while they are using their computers.

Grid computing is yet another method to increase the power of data mining. Indeed, if the data is associated with machine-readable descriptions of significance and meaning, then grids can be made even more powerful; the so-called 'semantic grid' promises to allow greater and more effective automation of the coordination of resources to solve large-scale problems.[103]

Amalgamating databases

A database is a collection of organised or structured data. The structuring of data has some disadvantages, notably that the categories used for organising the data might be hard to map onto our perceptions. Filling in forms is often extremely annoying because one gets asked questions that don't seem to apply. For instance, someone collecting personal data might ask for annual income graded into separate bands (under $10,000, $10,000-$20,000, and so on), but a self-employed person might receive a highly variable amount of money each year, and may find it hard to put him or herself into any one of these bands. The information one puts on such forms goes straight into a computer where fine gradations and special cases will gum up the works, so the end result is that the filigree details of our lives are lost.

But the big advantage to pre-existing and rigid structures is the facilitation of efficient searching, ranking and other types of querying of the data. Once data is structured, one can mine interesting relationships out of it more easily. The cost is some inaccuracies in the information caused by cramming it into the pre-existing formats, but these pale into insignificance compared to the extra value that one can put on data by being able to get knowledge (useful information) out of it.

There is an extra possibility that allows even more value to be extracted, which is that one can put structured data together, so that, in effect, one gets a single large distributed database which can be queried in the normal way. That does not sound like much of an advance – after all, why not simply query all the databases one by one?

The answer is that different databases work on different principles, and often have different categories and terms for the same things. Even if not, to get information out of a group of databases would require several carefully worked out queries; it is not impossible to extract information from a group of databases, but it is difficult. Amalgamating databases renders distributed querying *practical*. And although many things are possible with computers in theory, it is practicality that counts.

For instance, in January 2007, the UK government mused aloud about reforming 'overzealous' data protection laws which prevented ministries sharing information about its citizens. There were no plans to increase the quantity of information being collected, only to allow sharing between agencies. The result was meant to be easier for citizens – one minister cited the case of a family which had to make 44 phone calls to inform the government of a death.[104]

This is all very well (though as data about the dead is not protected, there is no reason why government departments couldn't pass that information on). But sharing information across government databases will dramatically increase governmental powers – otherwise the UK government wouldn't have proposed it. Merely amalgamating the tax and benefits databases will enable the government to discover all sorts of discrepancies – many of which will be innocent – that could prompt investigation.

One key point is often forgotten – government is not infallible. In fact, one of our best protections from totalitarianism is the relative incompetence of governments. Amalgamating databases could magnify the effects of incompetence. On an isolated database, misleading information from, say, an incorrectly filled-in form would probably be harmless. But linked into a network of databases, the error could propagate across several branches of government. If an income of £20,000 was accidentally recorded as £200,000, that affects very many potential interactions with government, and in combination with other pieces of information (e.g. that one paid £2,000 of tax last year, or that one claimed £5,000 of benefits) could be extremely damaging.

In private hands, amalgamated databases can be even more frightening. In the US in 1994, a young girl called Megan Kanka was brutally murdered by a convicted sex offender who lived across the street from her; in the aftermath of this awful event, a number of states, and eventually the federal government, enacted what have come to be known as Megan's laws, in honour of the victim. Megan's laws in effect oblige the authorities to reveal to a community the whereabouts of released sex offenders living in it.

With the relatively transparent government in the United States, this means that an awful lot of information is available about the offenders in one's neighbourhood. If one was suitably driven, one could collect all that information, but would have to look up several databases, which may require registration to access. Some of the databases might be paper-based. All in all, there would be quite an effort involved to put together the information required. But if all those databases were put together – and as we will see later on, the technology to do just that is now available – finding one's local rapist would be a trivial matter. And what is undeniably valuable to a concerned parent could also make feasible a whole new class of vigilante activity.

Natural language processing

Computers are pretty bad at understanding human motives and communications, and that is an important protection. When we use natural language in a digital medium (e.g. on a webpage), we preserve a bit of privacy because the computer, although it can search and copy the page, does not know what the page is about. It can't tell the difference between an admiring article about a government and a subversive one.

The usual way of searching is with keywords à la Google, but these don't tell you very much about what is in the document itself. A Google search for 'bush' produces 222,000,000 webpages, but the ordered list that results doesn't tell you whether this refers to one of the Presidents, the musician, a shrub, the metal lining of an axle-hole or merely a misprint for 'bash'. If the page does refer to a President, the search doesn't tell you which one, or whether it is pro, anti or neutral.

That is because natural language is not machine-readable; the computer does not understand what the page says. The language is structured according to the tenets of English, French or whichever language it is, but the information conveyed by the text is *not* structured, so the computer gets confused. However, greater computing power now does allow the development of statistical techniques to read texts and to extract the information structures from them. Such techniques (collectively called *natural language processing* or NLP) need very large corpuses of natural languages to learn from and some major computing power to make hypotheses about what the important structures are (both of which are available thanks to Moore's Law).

So, for instance, a sentence such as 'George D. Hay founded the Grand Ole Opry' is more or less meaningless to a computer, just a string of characters indistinguishable from 'Kelvin eats artichokes' or 'ailrghfaerghewodfdndf'. One can tell the computer, for an individual sentence, that 'George D. Hay' is a person, that 'the Grand Ole Opry' is an object, and that 'x invented y' is a certain relation between two things (and one can maybe even go further, telling the computer some possible inferences, such as that y did not exist before x invented it). But one cannot do that for every sentence, and anyway natural languages are too flexible for such an approach to be usable in general.

But a *statistical* analysis, if there is enough data (and the Web alone contains two thousand billion words), enables clever NLP programs to extract all the significant structures from sentences, with some training from a human operator. And that, in effect, enables the computer to turn a piece of plain text, unreadable by machine, into a machine-readable database. As with all these technologies, the benefits of NLP are large, but one of its effects is to open up previously opaque areas of discourse to view.[105]

MEMORIES FOR LIFE

One more area where Moore's Law has moved the goalposts is that of personal memory. The amount of information that an ordinary person can generate, and store, is now colossal. It is possible to store digital versions of life's memories in increasing quantities. As human-computer interaction specialist Alan Dix

once playfully noted, it takes 100 kilobits/second to get high quality audio and video. If we imagine someone with a camera
strapped to his or her head for 70 years, that will generate video
requiring something of the order of 27.5 terabytes of storage, or
about 450 60gb iPods.[106] And if Moore's Law continues to hold
over the next 20 years or so (admittedly a big if), we could store a
continuous record of a life on a device the size of a sugar cube.[107]

The ability to record memories, and store them indefinitely in
digital form in virtually unlimited quantities has been dubbed the
phenomenon of *memories for life*. This is an important area of interdisciplinary research; we will need to understand how it will affect
our social and political lives, and our psychological memories. We
also need knowledge about how best to design devices to enable
us to get the most out of these developments (as opposed to
simply drowning in the flood of information that will follow).[108]

But again, what might be an empowering or entertaining
development for many might double as a series of multiple
attacks on our privacy. After all, photographs and documents fea-
turing you may turn up in other people's memory banks. Intimate
photos of ex-girlfriends and boyfriends are often published mali-
ciously online (a Google search for 'ex-girlfriend nude photos' got
287,000 hits in July 2007, with 'ex-boyfriend nude photos' getting
271,000). You might easily appear in the background of a photo
or video clip taken by a complete stranger. One look at the video-
sharing website YouTube demonstrates that your eccentric
moments can be distributed around the world without your
knowledge or control. Yet again ease of storage combined with
computing power give us lots of information (good), but also
access to aspects of people's lives that were formerly private
(bad). Sometimes people give their privacy away, and sometimes

they surrender it. But sometimes they are innocent victims, in the wrong place at the wrong time, and it is very hard to protect privacy under such circumstances.

THE END OF PRACTICAL OBSCURITY

In this chapter, we have discussed a number of the technological advances that Moore's Law has made possible, including the decryption of encrypted information, data mining, e-science, amalgamating databases, natural language processing and memories for life. They are all important and useful technologies, and all dependent on massive computing power.

What they have in common is that they bring data out into the open, they make transparent (to machines) what was previously opaque. Much of the information they make available existed before, either implicitly, in coded form, or merely stored away and hard to get at. Privacy was preserved, before these technologies, by *practical obscurity*; in the days of distributed paper records, the effort of looking for information (that might not even be there) was usually too great to lead to any great abuses. A wrongly filed piece of information, to take one example, is as lost in a large repository as if the piece of paper it had been written on had been burned.[109]

This practical obscurity, a physical fact in the days of paper, is an important part of the delicate balance between our privacy, our need for information, governments' and corporations' need for efficiency, the law and technology. Moore's Law has been chipping away at practical obscurity. Our privacy laws tend to assume that information is a struggle to find; computing power may not change the principles involved in privacy protection very much, but it dramatically alters the *need* for protection.

CASE STUDY: SCIENCE, CRIME AND DATA

Big datasets are *de rigeur* now that data mining tools are so powerful. The ability to process giant quantities of data has transformed science. At the time of writing, the physics community is holding its breath for the flood of data that will flow from the Large Hadron Collider (LHC) at CERN in Switzerland, a big atom smasher designed to create enough information about high energy atomic collisions to provide evidence about the existence of some very exotic subatomic particles, such as the Higgs Boson whose existence is predicted by current physical theory but which has never been observed. The LHC is designed to produce 15 petabytes of information annually – that is a billion megabytes, which, if printed out, would need fifty million trees to be pulped and turned into paper. It is approximately equivalent to the amount of information produced in office documents across the world in one year, and will be about 1% of humankind's annual production of information.[110]

E-science, the conduct of science by amassing and analysing giant quantities of data, is an important research programme in many countries. Big computers and computing grids are set to work on the data, and there are many serious and interesting research issues to do with coordinating distributed computational resources, ensuring that the various computers trust each other with potentially sensitive data, and creating what are in effect virtual organisations to carry out e-science programmes. For example, the CombeChem project put in place a computational infrastructure (ranging from big number-crunching computers to electronic laboratory notebooks) to analyse various closely-related chemical compounds to determine their properties and work out how they might be used in the development of novel pharmaceutical compounds.[111]

So far, so good. After all, the Higgs Boson, elusive though it is, has few if any privacy concerns. But science also requires data about people, and people are concerned about privacy. Studies of drug trials (say) will involve the collection of data about people which may include lifestyle information about sexual preference, and genetic information about the probability that certain conditions will be inherited. This data is certainly more sensitive than the LHC's.

Indeed, the onward advance of science and medicine will involve the collection of information that goes beyond special-purpose datasets to document clinical trials or other experiments. Understanding the structure of the background population in great detail is now possible thanks to Moore's Law. Typically, experiments and analyses are performed using sampling methods and statistics; a random sample of a wider population is analysed, and statistics tells us the probability that the structure of the random sample reflects the structure of the population as a whole. If 44% of a sample is overweight, then given the sample size and the estimated size of the population, statistics will tell us, say, that it is 99% certain that between 41% and 47% of the population as a whole is overweight. As the sample size increases both absolutely and as a proportion of the population as a whole, then, if it is random, the structure of the sample is increasingly likely to reflect the structure of the population.

Moore's Law makes it possible to make the sample almost as large as the population itself. One recent innovation is the biobank, a repository of tissue or DNA samples, databases of medical information and test results. Biobanks are becoming increasingly important, partly because the increase in information they allow is useful in its own right, but also because medical research is coming to the realisation that patterns of disease and cure are more closely related to the individual than has previously been thought. Most pills and potions are of the 'one size fits all' variety, with one type of pill used to serve an entire population, but actually we are genetically and environmentally distinct, and it may be that individuals require individualised treatments for many conditions. But tailoring a cocktail of drugs for an individual requires far more knowledge about how our genes dispose us to resist and accept both the causes and treatments of disease.

Much of this biobanking is government-led. The UK Biobank began to extract information about the lifestyle and health of 500,000 volunteers in 2006, together with a blood and urine sample. Researchers can follow the progress of these half million to study the progression of cancers, diabetes, heart disease and Alzheimer's disease.[112] The Singapore Tissue Network was established in 2002 to archive tissue and DNA samples (both diseased and healthy),[113] and the Karolinska Institute in Sweden also hosts an archive of samples.[114] The Singapore Tissue Network allows donations and also includes clinical tests and trials, whereas the Karolinska Institute stores samples as a service for researchers, but also plans to follow 500,000 Swedes for 30 years with a similar mission to the UK effort. Indeed, Sweden has been a pioneer in biobanking, and possesses a blood or tissue sample from each of its citizens. Iceland, Quebec and Japan have also been assiduously collecting valuable blood and tissue samples for generations without creating much of a stir.

The problem, it goes without saying, is privacy. The various biobanks try to reassure donors that their samples will be safe. The UK tells us:

> Data and samples will only be used for ethically and scientifically approved research. Issues such as consent, confidentiality, and security of the data are guided by an Ethics and Governance Framework overseen by an independent council ....[115]

In Singapore, whose attitude to privacy is somewhat more relaxed than in Europe or the United States, we have:

> The Singapore Tissue Network is committed to following the highest standard for ensuring donor's rights for privacy and confidentiality. Our operating standards and policies are centered on informed consent where participants/donors engage in a dialogue with the party seeking the consent. All medical information is kept confidential by a system of sample coding and anonymization.
>
> We ensure that prospective donors understand that their donation is entirely voluntary and secondary in nature to their diagnosis.
>
> The tissue repository guidelines follow that of Singapore's Bioethics Advisory Committee, which is a panel of respected opinion leaders appointed by the Ministry to study the ethical, legal, and social issues arising from research on human biology. The BAC works closely with an international panel of advisors to develop and recommend policies to the Life Sciences Ministerial Committee of Singapore.[116]

While in Sweden:

> Ethics is essential in biobank-related research. Sample and associated data will only be used for ethically and scientifically

approved projects with strong emphasis on individual consent and information. Strong safeguards are maintained to prevent unauthorized access to samples and sensitive data.[117]

All very reassuring. Except that the Swedes also gerrymandered a loophole to extract important information from their national biobank as part of a crime investigation. The crime was a major one, the murder of foreign minister Anna Lindh by a psychotic knifeman in a Stockholm department store in 2003, but confidentiality was clearly breached. Blood and hair found at the scene of the crime were matched against the murderer, via his record in the biobank. There was other evidence (including CCTV footage, a previous criminal record and a history of severe psychiatric problems), and indeed the murderer confessed to relatives and friends. The police were shadowing him long before they arrested him. It is a key point about a giant database such as a biobank that it can't be used to make random searches. If you want to match one sample against everything in the biobank (whose DNA is this?), the search, even on today's powerful computers, would be too time-consuming and error-prone. But if you were matching the sample against a very small number of entries in the biobank (does the DNA belong to this particular person?), then the matching is much more tractable. It was supposedly the case that the biobank was off-limits to criminal investigators, but when push came to shove, biobank officials felt they could not refuse the police request in the face of this very high profile case. Later, Swedish law was changed temporarily to allow DNA samples to be used to identify Swedish victims of the Asian tsunami of 2004.[118] In each case, practice breached a clear understanding about the way that biobank information would be used.

Our intuitions about the public good, and about the importance of keeping a promise of confidentiality, may or may not be challenged by either of these two unforeseen uses of biobank information. One method of getting round the issue is to keep the information anonymously. After all, what matters is that tissue, blood and DNA samples are known to come from the same person, and that the person's lifestyle, age, sex and medical history are correctly logged and associated with the right samples. The identity of the person is not strictly necessary. That would clear up a number of privacy concerns; the murderer of Anna Lindh could not have been identified via the DNA he left on the murder weapon, and the tsunami victims could not have been identified. Other potential uses of a biobank are ruled out by anonymisation: for instance, people with a newly-discovered genetic predisposition to certain conditions could not be alerted.

UK DNA DATABASE

Some scientific databases cannot be anonymised, because their aim requires the retention of names – perhaps most obviously crime-fighting databases. The UK government's DNA database, set up in 1995, contains about four million records, over half a million of which were taken from children under 16. The 2003 Criminal Justice Act allows samples to be taken at arrest for a recordable offence (which includes being drunk and disorderly, and taking part in an illegal demonstration, for instance), not at charge time. Samples are kept permanently regardless of whether the donor was ever charged or convicted. 37% of black men in the United Kingdom are represented in the database. Tens of thousands of children who have never been charged with an offence are in there too. There are clear privacy concerns with the database, but on the other hand clear value too: every week 1,600 DNA matches link together either a criminal and a crime scene, or two crime scenes. The inventor of DNA profiling has argued that a trusted third party should be custodian of the database, to prevent police misuse, and also, much more radically, that the entire population should be on it, to prevent discrimination against over-represented groups.[119]

5

IT'S THE LINKS, STUPID: THE INTERNET, THE WORLD WIDE WEB AND PRIVATISED SPACES

Creation, definition and defence of rights to privacy are the traditional methods of enshrining our instincts into law. However, the development of technology, particularly the Internet and the World Wide Web, is an important backdrop – the Web is a highly decentralised system, and it is clear that the increase it affords in freedom of expression is offset by a corresponding difficulty in preventing people from revealing and disseminating private information. The architecture of the Web is intended to allow the expression and linking of information without any central control. The Web is not hierarchically organised; indeed it is extremely democratic, in that any page can be linked immediately, with no intermediaries, to any other page that the author considers relevant. But what is good for democracy is bad for gatekeeping. The Web is not particularly transparent: it isn't straightforward to discover all the links to one's information resources, or all the pieces of information that have been published about one. Neither are Web authors very accountable. Copying information is extremely easy, as is distributing it – the whole purpose of the Web is to be a knowledge-sharing infrastructure – and the fluidity of identity on the Web helps preserve anonymity. None of that is to denigrate the benefits of the Web, which has transformed the world in the last 15 years, largely for the better. But an architecture that supports the serendipitous reuse of information in new and unexpected contexts has obvious privacy implications.

Legal scholar Jack Balkin has written of the great achievements in the promotion of free speech in the twentieth century, and the way these have been affected by technology.

> The system of free expression is produced through the synergy of (1) government policies that promote popular participation in technologies of communication, (2) technological designs that facilitate decentralized control and popular participation rather than hinder them, and (3) the traditional recognition and enforcement of judicially created rights against government censorship. The last of these ... is the great achievement of the twentieth century. Nevertheless, I believe that in the long run it will be recognized as only one leg of a three-legged stool that supports the system of free expression. The other elements will increasingly move to the foreground of concern as it becomes clear that they are necessary to the promotion of a democratic culture.[120]

This is an important argument, and in many ways the situation with respect to privacy is the complete inverse. Popular participation, technological design and enforcement of rights together provide the context for the politico-legal understanding of privacy, but the measures that have shored up free expression have tended to *erode* privacy. In short, as participation increases, privacy tends to decrease. The original users of the Internet and the Web were nerdy academic computing types (including the present authors), and the original idea of the Web was as a forum for exchanging academic papers, in Berners-Lee's words, 'to allow information sharing within internationally dispersed teams, and the dissemination of information by support groups.'[121] This information-exchange idea, modelled on Vannevar Bush's idea of the Memex,[122] presupposes a relatively focused body of users for whom the sharing of information is key to the common good. In academic research, the more available information is, the easier it is to get things done, to make progress. Copyright, subscriptions, and the hoarding of information and data tend to restrict general progress (even if some individual reputations are boosted by them), so the Web was intended to facilitate – and is still being engineered to facilitate – information sharing.[123] Information's value on the Web is created by abundance, not scarcity. But when the Web expanded to include various perfectly legitimate activities – e-commerce, banking, gaming – and others not-so-legitimate – pornography, gambling – different architectures were suddenly required. The anonymity, democracy and ability to copy that made the Web a success don't look quite so wonderful when one's bank account is online, or one's ex-boyfriend is in possession of compromising digital photographs.[124]

Similarly, the basic architecture of the Web is designed to facilitate copying and democratic linking.[125] This means that although it is true that cyberspace can be regulated and that architectural decisions will constrain online behaviour in wide-ranging and quite political ways,[126] it is not a *trivial* matter to create an architecture that protects online privacy while retaining the important invariants of the decentralised information-sharing Web experience.

The Internet, and particularly the Web, are odd sorts of spaces, neither fully public nor fully private, and are a good example of a particular intermediate kind of space where public and private aspects mingle that emerged during the Enlightenment alongside an increasing understanding and theorising of commerce and trade. Such intermediate spaces are essential in modern societies, but make different and complex demands upon us.

Privatised spaces

The eighteenth century was the period when theoreticians began to develop the liberal idea of the public marketplace, where interactions and exchanges would take place in good faith between people whose interrelations were governed by instrumental reasons calculated on the basis of 'enlightened self-interest'. This mirrored architectural, economic and technological changes that meant that less work was done within the home (and so fewer people had to entertain buyers and clients in their own limited living spaces),[127] and correspondingly more work done in public offices, factories and exchanges. The development of a public yet privatised space went alongside the creation of media that were independent of the state but nevertheless reserved for themselves the right to comment, publicly, on public affairs (at least partly because of the state's giant influence on the conduct of business and trade).[128] Adam Smith (1723–90) was the most important thinker here,[129] together with fellow scions of the Scottish Enlightenment based in Edinburgh, such as David Hume and Adam Ferguson. This public space, viewed as an important foundation for social prosperity, was abstracted for the first time from other types of interaction, an abstraction which suggested the complementary concept of a private space.

For it was obvious, certainly to thinkers such as Smith and Hume, that these instrumental relationships did not exhaust human interaction.[130] Many of our relationships (notably friendships, loving relationships and family relationships) are not instrumentally driven, and so are not covered by Smith's theory of markets and the 'invisible hand'. One of the things that Smith was worried about was that, prior to his theory, these two types of relationship were mixed together – commercial decisions were made on the basis of uncommercial reasons (such as friendship – one might give special prices to one's friends, to the detriment of the market as a whole), while friendship itself was often seen in instrumental terms.

The idea that there was a public/private dichotomy now seemed somewhat less convincing. The geometry appeared to be three-sided. There seemed, in other words, to be three separate spaces, broadly conceived;[131] different theorists drew the various lines in different ways, but the general thrust of the tripartite distinction appeals to many of our intuitions. There was an unambiguously *private* realm of intimacy and individualism. Publicly defensible reasons for actions need not be given. Others' rights of interference were tacitly downplayed, although claims of morality and religion were believed by many to legitimise interference. Then, there was an unambiguously *public* realm of citizenship and active participation in collective decision-making, the realm of the *polis*. Here, action had to be publicly justifiable, and its reasons should not include benefits to the agents. In this realm, one thought and calculated on behalf of the public good, though there may be disagreements over what constituted the public good. This realm was usually highly regulated. But in the middle was a *third* realm, of public life, sociability and public opinion. In this area of unplanned encounter, one would be expected to put forward one's own views and to make one's voice heard. Equally, as the aim was at least sometimes to persuade others of one's views, actions in this third realm might be motivated by personal and selfish interest, but some of the reasons for actions would be deliberately couched in publicly-accessible terms.

This third area of sociability can be conceived as either public or private, depending on what it is contrasted with. Compared with the public, collective, decision-making realm, it is a private space – reasons are private, and actions need not be motivated towards improving the general lot of society. In the social world, there is no imperative to sacrifice one's own interests for the good of others. But contrasted with the private space of intimacy, it is an area of public interactions, of visibility, where one would expect to be seen and could not object to being reported. Consider a seminar going on in a lecture theatre in a university building: is the seminar public or private? Is the lecture theatre a public or a private space? Compared to the foyer, it is private. Someone who came in and began to eat sandwiches would be admonished 'Don't do that, this is a *private* meeting.' Compared to the toilet, it is public. Someone who came in and began to apply athlete's-foot powder would be admonished 'Don't do that, this is a *public* meeting.' But if the two transgressors compared notes, they would be wrong to detect contradiction between the two admonishments. It is neither fully public nor fully private, a *privatised* space.

This intermediate public/private social realm has been seen as essential for creating the public opinion required for the

development of the modern state, with its democratic tenden-
cies.[132] That does not mean development is uniform. In Britain,
the coffee houses where men of business would meet to chat,
gossip and share intelligence became the banks and insurance
companies that drove business, trade and the industrial revolution, whereas the free-ranging debates in the Parisian *salons* led
directly to revolution of a more thoroughgoing and destructive
sort. States where the public realm invades or has invaded the
social, for instance totalitarian dictatorships which suppress free
debate and discussion, find it very hard after the totalitarian era
has ended to switch to democratic structures, often because a privatised realm has not emerged and therefore there is no forum for
constructive, sometimes bad-tempered debate which does not
prevent the work of government from continuing.[133]

The Web is one of these interesting privatised spaces, independent of government, where the public good is only one motive
for action, but hardly private in the intimate sense. One must
expect to be seen, read and copied. One makes an appearance.

Spatial privacy

We have talked a great deal about privacy in terms of control of
information about oneself. Indeed, the Internet and the Web are
entirely concerned with the traffic of information. But another
kind of privacy is *spatial privacy*, with which people have a space
into which they can retreat in order to live the intimate portion of
their lives and to perform the uninterrupted reflection that they
will need in order to take maximal advantage of their autonomy.
For most people, the obvious example is their home. In Western

democracies, the number of others who are entitled to enter without permission is very small,[134] and those entitlements are operative only under very stringent conditions and after a court has heard arguments about the case.

Spatial privacy usually refers to a real space in the world, but the online world can also be seen as a metaphorical space.[135] An owned website is one example of an online space which one should be able (*modulo* libel laws etc) to populate with content. Another interesting type of online space is the browsing path one follows; one sits at one's computer and follows a chain of links, downloading pages as one goes. Indeed, virtually everything that a user of the Internet does involves interacting with a 'server', which retains the information about what was requested in a file called a 'server log'. The server log is required in order for the server manager to analyse the patterns of Internet traffic and therefore to keep the server as efficient as possible. But in effect the server log is a trace of the pages one has visited, the people whom one has emailed, and so on. Server logs, it should be pointed out, do not collect user-specific information; they are not surveillance devices. But the infrastructure does render such surveillance possible. One's own computer, of course, also retains such traces, as does one's Internet service provider.

But the Internet is an odd kind of space anyway. It occupies the privatised zone between public space and intimate space, and one is, to an extent, operating in public as well as in private. A webpage is often, if not always, meant to be seen by others, even if ownership of the content is private; to that extent, it is somewhat like a billboard. The trail of one's Internet interactions is a different and somewhat more difficult idea. The pages one downloads are public, but equally one's download is not necessarily a public act, and may also depend upon the relative privacy of the offline space which hosts the interaction. There is a great difference between reading a webpage at home, in an Internet café or at work (and of course in the last case the transaction might well be paid for by one's employer). If one interacts with the online space in a private offline space, then that is one thing, but equally if one is sitting in the view of others, for example in a café, then the nature of the privacy one might expect is surely reduced. Records will automatically be kept of one's Internet use no matter what, but the *physical* location of the interaction (not a factor often mentioned) also seems of importance.

Privatised space invasion

How are the privatised spaces of the Internet and the Web constructed? What is allowed, and what constrained, by the architecture? Each computer connected to the Internet has a numerical code signifying its place in the network called an 'IP address'. The link between the IP address and the computer is made by a company which sells access to the Internet, the Internet Service Provider (ISP). Most ISPs assign IP addresses 'dynamically' – that is, they 'own' a slew of addresses, and one's computer is assigned one of these IP addresses purely for the period of the session. All information sent to you is sent to the IP address, and so anyone interacting with you must know the address; the basic mechanism of the Internet is that information to be sent from one computer to another is chopped up into conveniently-sized packets marked with the destination's IP address, and sent via a series of computers. The IP address identifies one's ISP, and often one's nation or even city of residence. If an IP address is associated permanently with a computer (as opposed to being assigned dynamically), then the address will even identify that computer.

IP addresses and ISPs are essential for the Internet to run, but there are other ways of using the Internet infrastructure to threaten online privacy. We have already discussed cookies, little pieces of information that get passed back from one's machine to a website, usually for perfectly harmless reasons. It is possible that cookies could be used to extract somewhat more information than is perhaps desirable – allowing a profile of the user to be built up, for example. Most browsers allow the user to manage interactions with cookies, although disabling them completely does limit one's use of the Web. Cookies aren't usually a serious problem. More important is a type of malware called 'spyware'.

Spyware is software dropped onto one's computer specifically to collect information without informed consent. As a piece of software, it has to be installed on the machine (which obviously an informed user would not wish to do), so spyware and other malware is usually concealed in something else, such as an email attachment; hence it is always unwise to click on a file when one does not know its provenance. Once installed, spyware can collect information from a variety of sources. It can store the user's browsing history, log individual keystrokes, or search through documents on the hard disc. Most spyware is for commercial purposes, intended to target spam email marketing, or change one's Web browser homepage (commercial spyware is often called 'adware'). But there is always the risk of spyware's being intended for criminal purposes, to gather passwords or bank details. Setting up proprietary anti-spyware security programs and keeping them up to date will usually be sufficient to keep the threat at bay.

People can also be tricked by fake websites or emails, a practice known as 'phishing'. Here the user receives an email, apparently from a *bona fide* bank or store, which persuades him to part with important personal details, often on the spurious grounds of a 'security check'. Approximately two million Americans gave away details to spoof websites to the year ending August 2006, resulting in losses to American banks of about $2.8 billion (about twice what the Iraq War costs the British government annually).[136] In a recent experiment, good phishing sites could fool 90% of the experimental group, and the group made mistakes some 40% of the time. The cues that the Web browser gives to help the user were sometimes ignored: 23% of the participants didn't look at either the status bar, address bar or security indicators. Lack of knowledge was a key problem, and education about computing systems seems to be sorely lacking. For instance, a URI such as www.ebay-members-security.com does *not* belong to www.ebay.com, even though they share a common set of strings; phisherpholk choose URIs like the former because they can be associated in the minds of the unwary with trustworthy websites such as the latter. Many users are unaware that the little padlock in the browser indicates that the page has been delivered securely; the same padlock in the body of the webpage (a common phishing trick) indicates nothing.[137]

THE WEB

Phishing is made possible by a vital part of the Internet, the World Wide Web, perhaps the most complex technological development in the history of mankind, which has transformed life, certainly in the developed world and increasingly elsewhere, in all sorts of ways. Originally conceived – like many of the technologies we have discussed in this book – as a tool for aiding scientists, allowing them to share information and documents, it has now become the locus for shopping, banking, meeting friends, dating, gambling, political activism, entertainment and gossip, to name but eight. For most of us it is the attractions of the Web in particular that entice us into cyberspace. Indeed, it has even been argued by anti-capitalists that the Web is the snake in the techno-garden of Eden, the agent of the loss of cyber-innocence.

> This transformation of the Internet from a virtual state of nature to a virtual pluralistic civil society has been facilitated by technological innovation. What is now popularly known as the Net is dominated by the World Wide Web... No longer was the Net a text-based system centred around dialogic communication and postings, an anarchic mélange of newsgroups and listservs and gopher sites. It had become a multimedia phenomenon of linked Web sites where search engines, advertisements, commerce and entertainment existed alongside the traditional text-based Net of old.[138]

Whereas the Internet was a conversation, the Web is a set of one-sided presentations.

> A presentation is based on a script, can be repeated without losing its essential qualities, and, what is most important, is intended for an audience. While there are brilliant conversationalists, conversation is essentially egalitarian. Presentations ... value talents and demand expertise. They are inegalitarian...

An audience is ordinarily not expected to participate in the presentation. They are there to be entertained, informed, inspired, awed, manipulated, energized and the like. The real class division in Cyberspace is between the Webmasters and the Surfers.[139]

However that may be, the Web has meshed so smoothly with both the Internet and the patterns of daily life because of its design, an extremely simple platform of standards that allows ever more baroque structures to be built on top of it. Vanilla-flavoured at the bottom of the glass, it transmutes into weirder and more wonderful flavours, unpredicted and indeed unpredictable. The solidity of the foundation, in stern-sounding protocols and formalisms such as TCP/IP, HTTP, HTML and so on, allows the development of the Web as a revolutionary decentralised information structure.

ARCHITECTURE, IDEOLOGY AND LINEAR ALGEBRA

The Web's architecture is extremely simple. It is made up of 'formalisms' that allow the representation of information, and 'protocols' which govern the interactions between agents and the communication of the information. The central items in the system are 'resources', which are identified by Uniform Resource Identifiers (URIs). The URI is the text that appears in one's Web browser, such as 'http://en.wikipedia.org/wiki/Hypertext_Transfer_Protocol', which refers to a resource which is a piece of information, the description of the Hypertext Transfer Protocol in the English version of the online encyclopaedia Wikipedia.

URIs are based on structured definitions called 'schemes'; the Hypertext Transfer Protocol (HTTP) is perhaps the most common URI scheme, and is a method to transfer information around the Web. An HTTP URI can be identified by the 'http://' at the beginning. There are several other schemes, of which the file transfer protocol FTP, and the email scheme MAILTO are perhaps most often met.

A resource can be anything identifiable. If the resource is a piece of information (for instance, a file containing the text of this book), then it can, in principle, be put on the Web and retrieved from it. But other resources are just 'identifiable' from the Web, without being retrievable. So this book might be given a URI, but not actually be available on the Web; nevertheless making it identifiable by giving it a URI allows people to share information about it, reason about it, or even (if you would be so kind) to buy it.

Each aspect of the Web's architecture is intended to have minimal effects on other aspects. Hence the architectures underlying identification, representation and interaction are separate, and one can change the representation scheme of one without having to change the others. The system as a whole is therefore very flexible.[140]

Nevertheless, despite the basic nature of Web architecture, the way it is designed is an important determinant of what is possible online. In other words, there is a lot of power being dispensed by the geeks in charge.[141] In particular, the principles of the 'founding fathers' of the Internet and the Web, liberty to link to whoever one wishes, and to say whatever one wishes, need not always be enshrined in the Web. It can be a tool of control as well as one of free expression, if those in charge of architecture design choose to make it so. Underlying the Web is a basic liberal assumption that discussion, argument and the presentation of opposing views are the best ways to achieve consensus and the best outcomes; the Web could not be more liberal if it had been designed by John Stuart Mill,[142] which has disappointed more radical thinkers.

> While those working on the cutting edge might still see the Internet as a wide-open frontier, it has taken on the characteristics of a settled territory. The utopian vision of a worldwide agora which would revitalize democracy has to confront the harsh reality of lawsuits and regulations, of commerce and entertainment, of political parties, organized interest groups and political activists, and most importantly, of masses of bored and indifferent citizens.[143]

On the other hand, there is very little information online that one can now say is off-limits. Virtually all information that appears in a privatised space such as the Web is regarded by many as fair game. There has been, thanks to democracy, liberalism and postmodernism, a flattening of hierarchies of discourse. Nowadays, commentators are much less likely to argue that gossip is a bad thing, that one's private life is not a fit subject of interest for the layman. Extraordinary numbers of webpages are filled with tittle-tattle about unknowns who appear on *Big Brother*, for instance, but the idea that such gossip should be discouraged is very unfashionable. Even those who dislike *Big Brother* would be wary of arguing that such gossip should be banned, though this was a key point for Warren and Brandeis.

> Each crop of unseemly gossip, thus harvested, becomes the seed of more, and, in direct proportion to its circulation, results in the lowering of social standards and of morality. Even

gossip apparently harmless, when widely and persistently circulated, is potent for evil. It both belittles and perverts. It belittles by inverting the relative importance of things, thus dwarfing the thoughts and aspirations of a people. When personal gossip attains the dignity of print, and crowds the space available for matters of real interest to the community, what wonder that the ignorant and thoughtless mistake its relative importance. Easy of comprehension, appealing to that weak side of human nature which is never wholly cast down by the misfortunes and frailties of our neighbors, no one can be surprised that it usurps the place of interest in brains capable of other things. Triviality destroys at once robustness of thought and delicacy of feeling. No enthusiasm can flourish; no generous impulse can survive under its blighting influence.[144]

It is next to impossible to get away with such elitism nowadays, and even those who try disagree drastically about what social or moral standards we should have and are departing from in our unseemly gossiping. Hence, in a chaotic and argumentative online world, where very little information is deemed beyond the pale or too unimportant to be reported, and where the protection for individuals is thought by some to be inadequate, and certainly after the fact (requiring the harmed person to sue after the damage has been done), debate about privacy will continue.

It is possible to encrypt information on the Web, thereby protecting privacy. For instance, HTTPS is a URI scheme based on HTTP which includes an encryption mechanism based on a public key infrastructure, allowing information to be moved around on the Web relatively safely. Many secure sites, such as banking sites, use the HTTPS protocol, and often a password is required to get onto them. One way to avoid a phishing attack is to ensure that the URI displayed in the browser is an 'HTTPS' URI; this means that the information you hand over is genuinely encrypted.

Linking, which is supported by the structure of the Hypertext Markup Language (HTML) used for structuring text and other types of content in webpages, is a vital part of the Web experience, as are other HTML-enabled possibilities, such as copying and imitating. The idea, as we mentioned before, is the *reuse* of information. The way that digital media are created allows new documents to be created not only afresh, but from the old. Comments and metadata can be added to other people's work (even in online newspapers, articles are often followed by a long column of comments), and Internet communication thrives on the appropriation and reuse of other people's work.[145] But if the rules for HTML were changed, that whole appropriative model would be altered. The formalism creates the possibilities; there is nothing inherently imitative about decentralised discourse such as we find on the Web.

One key aspect of the Web is the ability to find the information one needs. In the beginning, one had to remember complex addresses, but HTML which allows pages to link to other pages via the blue *hyperlinks*, and clever search engines like Google, now allow interesting content to be found, if not perfectly at least pretty efficiently in a very short space of time. There are still problems with finding non-text items such as video and photographs, since they don't always come with keywords to aid the search. Nevertheless, taken all in all the Web is a very efficient storehouse of information.

Indeed, Google is perhaps the most elegant and well-known surveillance engine on the planet. It routinely scans and indexes pretty well most of the Web pages in existence; about ten billion in English at the time of writing. It then constructs an index of those pages and allows anyone with a Web browser to find content they are interested in on any of those pages. If we look briefly at its technology and the challenge it overcame, it should help us appreciate that even in the age of petaflops and petabytes it is still possible to survey most of what is out there. We have yet to transcend our own capabilities to observe our own behaviour.

In the 90s the sheer number of pages appearing on the Web became a challenge. How were we to find what was interesting and relevant to an individual? At the time search engine methods relied on finding and ranking pages by word count. But this was becoming more and more problematic. It was estimated that 95% of Web pages written in English only used 10,000 words of the language. This meant that searches based on word counting were returning more and more of what users regarded as irrelevant content. The insight behind Google was effectively to ask the Web itself to rank the importance of pages. The scientific elegance was the production of an analysis to do this; one moreover that could be implemented or engineered efficiently.

The insight was that the importance of a page is best understood in terms of the number and importance of pages linking to it. Each page on the Web is therefore assigned a measure of importance called its PageRank – when you type a term into Google it presents the pages containing that term in order of their PageRank. The problem is that this is an essentially circular definition – the importance of a page is determined by the importance of pages linking to it, whose importance is also determined by the importance of pages linking to them. The analysis of the problem that Google's founders Page and Brin developed exploited an elegant representation and encoding of the problem as well as ingenious methods to avoid a variety of problems encountered along the way.

At any moment in time the Web will contain N Web pages. We can represent the connectivity structure of the Web by a $N \times N$ matrix C. If a page i links to another j then $c_{i,j} = 1$, if not then $c_{i,j} = 0$. The ranking of any page r_i is entirely defined by this matrix. We can apply increasingly sophisticated rules to this matrix and these are embodied in the Google Page Rank formula. The essence of these rules is that firstly, the ranking of a page should grow with the number of links to it. Secondly, the ranking should be weighted by the ranking of each page linking in (i.e. if a highly-ranked paper links to your page, that is better than being linked to by a page with a low rank). Thirdly, pages that link in should contribute less the more links they have to other pages. The challenge is that the matrix representing the Web of just English pages is on the order of 10,000,000,000 rows. This is a large matrix and most of it is full of 0's. The genius of Google was to apply some fundamental principles of linear algebra to this matrix – reducing it to a so-called eigenvector – a vector containing a rank r_i for each page of the Web. This is computed using a method that initially proposes a vector then repeatedly adjusts it until when multiplied with the Web matrix reproduces its structure as determined by the rules above.[146]

The Web facilitates information flow. But there are obvious problems with this. In particular, there is little *transparency* or *accountability*. It is hard to discover how information is being used, and hard to hold people to account for any harm they do.[147] It is, of course, an aspect of free speech that transparency and accountability should be limited, and the ability to say more or less what one wants (within limits) is enshrined in the American constitution. There is an important contradiction in liberalism, which is that freedom (particularly freedom of speech) is prized, but equally so is privacy, so what do you do when someone uses their freedom of speech to breach someone's privacy? We should not be surprised to find this contradiction imported into an impeccably liberal technology like the Web.

First, information about one can be passed around more or less willy-nilly at the moment. There are certain websites that are designed to undermine privacy, from offender-tracking websites, to pornographic and semi-pornographic voyeur sites, to sites run by animal rights fanatics listing the private addresses of those involved in the supposed abuse of animals. It is the serendipitous reuse of information that often causes the problem; privacy is often compromised not by the publication of the information *per se*, but because it is linked to other significant contexts. Two pieces of information about a person might individually be harmless, but less so if linked. One's address is a piece of public information, available from the phone book or the electoral roll. One's job is similarly hardly a state secret. But put the two together, and someone with a vendetta against a company could put unwarranted pressure on an individual employee. With information, context is all, and linking is potentially a serious issue.

Secondly, sometimes we simply want to keep information private. Emails to friends, credit card details, artistic creations for which we hold copyright: we want to restrict access to all of these. One obvious way to do that would be not to post the content on the Web, but then one loses all the advantages of email, e-commerce, and the huge audience for one's work that one can achieve online.

We should also briefly mention one other factor that will have an effect on Web privacy in the foreseeable future. In the developed world, the usual method of access to the Web is via a

PC and some kind of cable connection. But in the developing world, where all-purpose computers are expensive, and electricity and telecommunications infrastructure weak, many people are connecting to the Web using mobile devices, the so-called 'mobile Web'. The programs, interfaces and devices to facilitate this development are not yet fully in place – most Web content is designed to be read using a PC or laptop, or printed off on paper, not on a tiny mobile phone screen. Furthermore, most mobile connections are intrinsically unreliable ('I'm on the train!'). Nevertheless, the mobile Web is here to stay. This does mean extra privacy problems, as wireless transmission of information is somewhat easier to intercept than cable-based transmission. The development of standards for the mobile Web is at an early stage.

THE SEMANTIC WEB

Another development at the cutting edge of the Web is the Semantic Web.[148] This is a very different approach to the issues facing Web developers as its size and complexity has increased, and – like many digital technologies – is primarily designed to provide better instruments for scientific investigation. As with the World Wide Web, initially the aim of the Semantic Web was to promote the sharing of data, and to improve communications.

The World Wide Web is basically a medium for sharing documents, be they images, scientific papers, lists, reports, videos, spreadsheets or what-have-you, and its value has been demonstrated over and over again during the last fifteen years or so.

Naturally, information contained in documents is shared when the documents themselves are shared. But there are still several steps needed to extract the information in documents to make it usable.

For instance, suppose you search (probably on Google) for documents containing important keywords, and a particular document is first on the list. You download the document. Now you have to find the bit that has the information you need. You could read the document from top to bottom (and it could be quite long). You could search through it looking for particular text strings. It may even be that after all that work, the fact you were looking for was not in the document at all. Then you have to go back to the Google search list, download document number two, and so on.

Even once the fact is discovered, you are not out of the woods. The fact may be represented in an inconvenient form. It may be something simple, such as a measurement given in imperial units when you want it in the metric system. But it could be explained in a long piece of text that is somewhat hard to understand. Or it could be presented at the wrong level of abstraction (too detailed an account for your purposes, or not detailed enough). Or it could be presented in the wrong format. It could be a load of structured data presented in a text table, so that you can extract the data but you have to recreate the data structures yourself (and the table might have hundreds of rows and columns). There is no doubt that the World Wide Web has improved the lives of anyone who depends on timely access to information, but even once you have the very document you need, you still have plenty of work to do.

The Semantic Web is intended to take information-sharing to the next stage, by doing for data what the Web did for documents;

you should be able to harvest raw data from the Web and analyse it. It should be possible to amalgamate data from various sources, discover subtle links and relationships between them and tailor the results in the ideal way for your own purposes. The Web automated the collection of documents, and the Semantic Web should automate the extraction of information from them.

Typically, information inserted into documents would be tagged by the author to indicate what the information refers to, to give the information some *meaning* (hence, 'Semantic' Web). A normal document might contain a numeral, '6', say, but the computer can make no inferences about that – to the computer it is just an uninterpreted numeral. With the formalisms the Semantic Web makes available, and tools that can exploit them, the '6' can be given an interpretation. The computer might therefore be able to interpret the '6' as a temperature, or a house number, or the number of children a person has, or whatever. It could then perform some inferences over the document, if it were told something about those concepts. Furthermore, it could also work out when different terms referred to the same things. A computer with standard capabilities would see 'temp' and 'temperature' as two different strings, but with the Semantic Web one could tell the computer that they each refer to the same physical parameter.

The key insight of the Semantic Web is to use a new kind of Web language, the Resource Description Framework (RDF), to encode meaning in sets of triples; each triple being rather like the subject, verb and object of an elementary sentence. In RDF a document makes assertions that particular things (people, Web pages or whatever) have properties (such as 'is a sister of,' 'is the author of') with certain values (another person, another Web page). This structure turns out to be a natural way to describe a great deal of information. Subject and object are each identified by a Universal Resource Identifier (URI), which are familiar ways of identifying Web resources (the most common type of URI is the Web address). The predicates are also identified by URIs, which enables anyone to define a new concept, a new predicate, just by defining a URI for it somewhere on the Web.

Indeed, RDF needn't even be created explicitly. An award-winning Semantic Web application developed at the University of Southampton, CS AKTive Space, took information from the Web about computer science departments, and was able to work out automatically (with a bit of initial priming) what all the various departmental homepages were referring to, and represent that in RDF. It wasn't an easy task, and it involved a good deal of programming and headscratching, but the system did work.[149]

As a scientific tool, the Semantic Web shows great promise, and it also has enormous potential in any information-heavy exploit, including medicine, business and government. But it could also constitute a two-pronged attack on privacy. Firstly, the success of the Semantic Web, as with every other technology discussed in this chapter, will depend on the number of active users. Lots of people using it means lots of data available, and lots of interesting results, and then more users – a virtuous circle. Conversely, few users of the Semantic Web means little available data, which means uninteresting results, and fewer users. These technologies rely on 'network effects': many users now mean more users in future, and few users mean even fewer users.

The network effects of the World Wide Web began when people began routinely to publish their documents. So much has the online world changed since the Web came to fruition that it is hard to remember the pre-Web environment, but in those dark days people thought it strange that they might author a document and post it for all to see. If a company produced a paper on something, its managers would routinely assume that it was confidential, and that any potential reader should gain permission to view it. Even something as straightforward as a price list was usually confidential, and companies viewed the confidentiality of a complete catalogue as an important commercial tool. This instinctive information hoarding quickly broke down – after all, if your competitors published their price list, potential customers would be frustrated by your failure to follow suit. So gradually today's relatively open Web developed, and now documents are routinely posted online.

The Semantic Web is intended to do for data what the Web did for documents. This will mean people, organisations and firms routinely publishing their *data*, which is potentially much more sensitive. And the greater the gains from the Semantic Web, the more data will be published. This will, once more, be a huge change of corporate policy (which may or may not happen). But if it did, then information about one, which on the Web would be concealed at least to some extent in a document, would be available in raw form for others to see and use. The potential benefits to mankind would be enormous, but of course there would be risks to our privacy too. Another blow would have been struck to the notion of practical obscurity.

The second issue is the greater facility that the Semantic Web provides for discovery. Not only would more data be likely to find its way onto the Web, but it would be easier to query and make inferences about. The Semantic Web data structures in effect turn the Web into 'a kind of universal spreadsheet that is readable by computers as well as people', as computer scientist David de

Roure puts it.[150] That would make it possible to put together information from several websites, including ones where people reveal a lot about themselves, and analyse it much more deeply (and quickly, and automatically) than is currently the case.

For instance, one research project on the nascent Semantic Web took very basic information from a social network, and a database of academic papers, to discover potential conflicts of interest in the reviewing process for papers (if possible, the reviewing of academic papers by friends or colleagues of the authors should be avoided, because the objectivity of such reviews could not be guaranteed).[151] This is a very basic application of the idea of understanding an implicit social network from explicit relationships between people, and we can expect the idea to be honed still further in the future.

As with most technologies, the picture is not uniformly black. The ability to reason over data rather than documents might allow an *increase* in privacy in some respects because of the greater flexibility and intelligence of data-handling. For instance, with the WWW, if a document contains some sensitive information, then one of two things can happen. It can be given to a reader, in which case the sensitive information is revealed and privacy threatened. Or it can be withheld, in which case the document isn't used. But if Semantic Web technology allowed a finer-grained approach, then it might be possible to release the document in such a way that the sensitive data within it is 'blocked' for those readers who are not authorised to see it.

The policy-aware Web

The potential of the Semantic Web is very high. Of course, privacy laws will continue to operate, and privacy activists will remain properly vigilant. But the technologists themselves are also responding, and, as with privacy enhancing technologies, those with the remit to oversee the Web are trying to ensure that privacy protection is written into the technological foundations, below ground level as it were; the specification of the various layers of protocols that make up the Semantic Web explicitly includes a layer allowing the development of trusted connections between users. After all, if the network effects that are essential to the continuing development of the Web are to be realised, then it is essential that users are confident that their data or information will not be misused.[152]

As with digital technologies generally, it is important to make it possible for people or organisations to express their privacy policies understandably – ideally, in the case of the Semantic Web, machine-readably. It has to be borne in mind that the Web is a chaotic and decentralised place, with many different standards, languages, formalisms and purposes. A centralised approach will not work, so what might seem like the obvious idea of creating a system for registering and policing privacy policies that everyone would have to use to get on the Semantic Web is a non-starter. The Web thrives on decentralisation and the lack of constraints. Furthermore – to state the obvious – the Web is big, and any system that is intended to work at the scale of the Web needs to avoid the centralisation that tends to create bottlenecks in large-scale information structures.

Thinkers at the World Wide Web Consortium (W3C) hope to use the information-processing possibilities of the Semantic Web itself to allow systems to express and act on privacy preferences. Because the Semantic Web facilitates richer interactions with information, it should be possible to use those capabilities to express complex privacy policies, and for systems to reason about them. It should be possible to use Semantic Web formalisms to do the reasoning required to prevent the Semantic Web from invading everyone's privacy.

Daniel Weitzner and colleagues of the W3C call this the policy-aware Web,[153] which needs to meet three requirements. First, it needs to be transparent, so that both people and machines can discover and interpret the social constraints under which a resource wishes to operate. So the owner of a piece of information ought to be able to say that he wishes to sell it, but doesn't want it passed onto others. Similarly a buyer should be able to purchase the information on the express condition that he doesn't resell.

The second requirement of the policy-aware Web is that it must contain simple compliance mechanisms, so that all this privacy policy stuff goes on without most users knowing anything about it. The Web is the enormous social phenomenon it is because most users don't know anything about HTTP or HTML or SPARQL or whatever, and the policy-aware Web should continue that tradition – one has the right to be ignorant of what is under the bonnet. But even the most computer-illiterate users need to be confident that the privacy-supporting mechanisms will work.

And third, users should be accountable, so that when the rules are broken we should be able to identify the breach and take appropriate remedial action, whether the transgression was malicious or accidental.

However, for the first step, description should be stressed over enforcement. Enforcing policies which have not been properly expressed will be unfair, messy and fraught. The trick for the Web as it develops is to allow the description and dissemination of privacy policies to go ahead in the decentralised system. As the practice of creating and reasoning about privacy grows, then the policy-aware Web should serve as a platform for the development of enforcement systems that can work in the particular contexts that the future Web will create (the nature of which we can only guess at the moment). Initial infrastructures have been described, but the continued growth and development of the Web depends on progress in making users feel that their privacy is safe online.

6

MAN'S BEST FRIEND IS HIS BLOG: WEB 2.0

PROPERTIES OF A PRIVATISED SPACE: THE NEED FOR WRITERS

The Web, we have argued, is a privatised space midway between the completely public and the completely private, and such spaces are important for the formation of public opinion and the development of a constructive discourse about society. But during its great growth spurt between 1995 and 2005, the development of browsing tools that allowed people to *read* the Web outpaced that of *publishing* tools; the dialogue, in some areas, was dangerously close to being a monologue. But the publishing tools have caught up, driven largely by the creation of a new programming language AJAX (Asynchronous JavaScript And XML), which allows Web pages to be more responsive by exchanging small amounts of data between client and server, thereby allowing a page to be updated without rewriting the whole thing. Interactivity got a whole lot simpler. The balance between writers and readers has been redressed to a large extent by these tools; it is now much easier to get your opinions online.

Now that writers are online in force, the Web extends more deeply into private matters, while performance remains highly public. Blogging, for example, demonstrates the complex interaction of publicity and privacy. The blogger discusses something personally important; it may be the invasion of Iraq, it may be the latest Coldplay album, it may be the difficulty in getting a home streaking kit to work; momentous issues of the day or things incomprehensible outside a very small circle of acquaintances. The opinions expressed are the blogger's own, and the blogger is accountable to no-one (as long as the blog stays within the laws that govern any kind of speech). In that sense, a blog is very private. But equally these inconsequential private musings or rantings are intended to appear in public, to be read by people who have no conceivable relationship with the blogger. And the blogger's authority depends on whether what is said is influential or not; the blogger's position or qualifications are not relevant.

Jürgen Habermas distinguishes three factors that enabled the privatised space to bring political and institutional changes to wider society in the eighteenth century. First, rank counted for little (unlike at court); public opinion wasn't an egalitarian space, but was somewhat meritocratic, and you were distinguished by the quality of your arguments or the size of your fortune, not your aristocratic status. Second, the privatised space hosted discussions about problems of interest to the participants, which had not necessarily been certified as legitimate areas of debate by court or church. Third, there was a tacit assumption that a social gathering was embedded within a wider world of potential participation.[154] These three factors are replicated in the new media of the twenty-first century. Having said that, we should also note that, as participation in the eighteenth century privatised spaces required a certain level of manners and education, the same is true in the twenty-first century – a certain level of technical expertise and cultural savvy is needed to become a successful blogger. These spaces are not truly democratic as we would understand the term today, at least in so far as the digital divide persists.

Hannah Arendt also distinguishes a privatised space where politics goes on, a common world that brings us together but which transcends our actual relationships, spreading out beyond our life-spans, and which 'can survive the coming and going of the generations only to the extent that it appears in public',[155] although she argues somewhat more philosophically and less historically than Habermas.[156] Her characterisation also suggests three important parallels with new media. It is artificial and man-made; it has a spatial quality, so that political activities are located in a public space in which citizens can encounter each other; and action in the privatised space has its own ideals, so that we don't always act out of personal interests, but rather we are able to understand, articulate and defend some public interests.

Each characterisation of the privatised space that contributes to the public life of a realm or society tacitly assumes that discourse is two-way. People talk and write, and listen and read. Naturally, some people are more influential than others, and are listened to and read more than others. But everyone can have a say. Thanks to recent developments, the Web is a better, more dialogic, space.

Web 2.0

Web 2.0 is the name given to the highly participatory technologies that have augmented the Web. The name is applied broadly, and opinions differ as to whether it is a genuine development or a buzzword. It is characterised by a set of spaces that are highly popular and occupied by users' own content. A vital technology is the blog, where people write and post content for anyone to see. An audio or sometimes video version is the 'podcast', a media file that is downloaded and played back over an MP3 player. Some bloggers and podcasters are becoming extremely influential (although the most influential tended to have influence already in the old media world). Web 2.0 has produced networks of people, together with methods of search and discovery that are somewhat less formal than standard Web users might have become used to. The growth of Web 2.0 has come as something of a surprise to many, and although the term itself supposedly dates back only to 2003, it is now the coolest part of the Web.[157] The first blog appeared in 1997, and ten years later there were an estimated seventy million, according to blog-tracking site Technorati.[158] At this moment about 120,000 new blogs are being created each day – equivalent to 1.4 each second. An astonishing 57% of American teenagers create content for publication online.[159] Well-known Web 2.0 sites include:

- YouTube,[160] a free video sharing site that allows people to view video clips that have been uploaded by YouTube users.
- Flickr,[161] as YouTube except for photographs.
- del.icio.us,[162] for storing and sharing Web bookmarks.
- MySpace,[163] a social networking site which allows users to post personal details, blogs and other digital paraphernalia. Friends can link to other friends, which creates a network structure; one can follow links to find people whom one might like but currently doesn't know. After all, if A likes B, who likes C, who likes D, it might well be the case that A would like D, even if they have never met. Although this site

has yet to make money, it is one of the most popular sites online, with over 100 million accounts. As an illustration of how seriously the old media take the new, MySpace is owned by Rupert Murdoch's News International which acquired MySpace's previous owner for a cool $580 million.

- Wikipedia,[164] a surprisingly reliable online encyclopaedia whose content is created by users.

These well-known applications are trailblazers for any number of situations where people need to create and share content. Of course, much of the impetus is for social communication. Several social software sites are actually dating sites, usurping the role of dating agencies, but often with a new twist. mysinglefriend.com allows people to publicise the charms of their single friends (or, one supposes, themselves – 'I have a "friend" ').[165] Illicit Encounters is a 'discreet and confidential extra-marital dating service for women and men' – in other words, a site for people who want affairs. 'Whatever your reason, we can help. You may be locked in a loveless marriage, starved of attention and affection, partner away or too tired to pay you the attention you deserve, non-existent love life? Or just looking for some excitement in your life? But you don't want to end your marriage either. Here you can meet people just like you, in absolute confidence.'[166] Apparently, the male-female ratio is not quite even, despite women being allowed to join for free.[167] There is actually an affair-brokering site aimed directly at women, with the rather cutsie name of tummybutterflies.com, which sternly shouts 'WARNING: NOT EVERYONE IS SUITED TO HAVING AN AFFAIR. THEY ARE NOT AN ALTERNATIVE TO WORKING ON OR ENDING A MARRIAGE. NOT ALL

AFFAIRS HAVE A POSITIVE EFFECT ON A MARRIAGE, SOME CAN BE VERY DAMAGING. ALWAYS CONSIDER OTHER PEOPLE AND IF YOU ARE GOING TO HAVE AN AFFAIR, PLEASE SELECT YOUR PARTNER WISELY.'[168] No doubt these sites have serious privacy policies in place.

Where there is sex, scientists are sure to follow. They need to talk and share stuff too. One Web 2.0 site, myExperiment,[169] is explicitly based on MySpace, and is intended to allow scientists to collaborate, share experiences, expertise and information, and build up research groups. The scientists are learning from the teenaged denizens of MySpace how to develop virtual communities.

Another direction for Web 2.0 is to exploit what has been called 'the wisdom of crowds', the greater knowledge that a diverse group of people can bring to bear on a problem, rendering them (if their opinions can be appropriately aggregated) superior to experts.[170] For instance, the project A Swarm of Angels[171] is an 'open source' film project, intended to make an Internet-funded, crewed and distributed feature film. At the time of writing, it is hoping to persuade 50,000 people to donate $25, in return for which they get to provide input to the script and the film-making.

The extraordinary thing about these sites and others is that people spend a long time creating free content to be devoured by others. The scope for free-riding (reading but not writing, watching but not photographing) is vast (the Internet term for a free-rider is a 'lurker'), but even so this doesn't seem to restrict the creation or posting of content. This goes against many legal and political expectations about intellectual property.

In the days when information was carried around on paper, its value consisted in scarcity. You would have to pay for access to a book or an article, and reproducing that material often required buying a licence. The copyright owners were in effect granted a monopoly over the reproduction of their thoughts until well after their demise. It was thought that such monopoly provision was required in order to give people incentives to write at all – after all, why produce a piece of knowledge, or a story, or some music, if you would not profit from it? Actually, most evidence implied that this theory of selfish creativity was wrong. Great artists such as the composer Händel continued to produce work even when they were losing out to piracy. The number of books published continues to rise even as very few authors make money. And, as economist William Baumol has argued, the benefits to society from innovation (which are vast) tend not to be reflected in the rewards for the innovator; nevertheless, innovation is entrenched and systematic in capitalist economies.[172]

And when tools became available to allow people to create content *and publish it*, it turned out to be economic theory that was correct, and the psychological theory of selfish creativity was false. People produced stuff left, right and centre, most of which was the most utter tosh, but who cared? The resulting climate has proven difficult for defenders of intellectual property rights – the vision of multi-millionaire rock stars and record companies suing their fans and innovative nerds alike has not been edifying. Our understanding of the needs of the law will have to evolve. For instance, consider the following criticism of an attempt to draft a 'public privacy' law. The privacy law, it was argued:

> … would include as one determinant of liability an inquiry into whether images were disseminated or intended for dissemination to the general public. This factor would rarely, if ever,

apply to nonphotojournalists. Because ... [it has] the "inevitable effect" of singling out individuals engaged in expressive activity – reporters engaged in the publication or dissemination of photographs – [the proposal is] constitutionally suspect.[173]

This objection was no doubt valid at the time of writing in 1998, but is certainly not now. By 2005 Flickr alone had 245,000 members even though at that point it was still only available in the preliminary beta version.[174] The number of people demonstrably disseminating images to the general public now almost certainly dwarfs the number of photojournalists in the world by orders of magnitude.

In Web 2.0, even if people do not create online content, they can still interact with it. Much of the life of Web 2.0 is generated by *tagging*, categorising online content. The tags created by users according to their own often idiosyncratic ways of seeing the world, can be aggregated to show remarkable semantic and descriptive structures that can be highly informative for other users. The microscopic judgements of many users turn into macroscopic characterisations of content.[175] So, for instance, on YouTube, someone called ardentoctopus posted a video on 27 November 2006, showing his slide guitar cam – a man, presumably Mr Ardentoctopus, plays blues guitar for three minutes, filmed by a camera looking directly along the strings. The video has generated a large amount of comment, including fourteen video comments, and has been tagged with some key words: Blues, Slide, Yamaha, Guitar, Delta, Cam, Glass, Podcast, Raised, Nut. The significance of some of these, if not all, is obvious. Clicking on 'Blues' produces a list of alternative blues-related videos. The tags are often ambiguous; the tagging of Mr Ardentoctopus's video as 'Delta' obviously refers to the Mississippi Delta, and the tradition of blues therein that peaked with Robert Johnson, but a look at the other videos tagged with 'Delta' reveals a wide range, many of them performances by Australian actress and singer Delta Goodrem. However, putting the two tags together and looking for those tagged with 'Delta' and 'Blues' produces a musical feast for the enthusiast. Tagging is an important method of interacting with other people's content, and 28% of American Internet users had tagged something online as of December 2006. 7% of users will tag content on a typical day.[176] This enormous effort in tagging content online is one solution to the growing complexity of the Web where many people's judgements can be aggregated to categorise and search for content (the wisdom of crowds once more).

Web 2.0 is the place where the public aspect of the Internet really blurs with the private. There is nothing too mundane for bloggers to discuss, but many details of what is ordinarily thought of as private life are exposed and made public, as for example with this blog posted on 13th February, 2007, which records a melancholy evening in the English midlands.

> No cycling today and no good luck routine either. Although I suppose I did get to indulge last night. I'm on the bus because I'm off out in Derby for beer and curry tonight. The bus used the scenic route, through Borrowash, Spondon and Chadd, didn't help though. I was still late for work.
>
> My mate is giving up football (again) at the end of the season. I think mainly due to Leeds imminent relegation but also bizarrely because of Sky's withdrawal of Sky Sports News as a free channel. Awful channel, good riddance.

He also whinges about blind referees, overpaid footballers, inflated prices, poor quality football etc etc.

He does have a point but I point out that he doesn't in fact pay the inflated prices because he doesn't actually go to games! I think it's also a myth that football has ever been high quality and I quite like the blind refs, as it annoys all the overpaid footballers.

After work, I meet up with a couple of friends from my now distant school days in Derby. Have a couple of Triple Hop's 4.0% in the Brunswick. Then we go to the Shalimar for a curry. We have some money off vouchers. Have Lamb Madras, nice and spicy but rather tasteless. Cheese Naan is good. Have a pint of Cobra 5.0%. We spend a good night reminiscing. I have no watch at the moment and forget the time. End up running for the bus.

Get to the bus stop and the bus isn't there, so either it's late or I've missed it. Then, as I walk to the stop, I see it, skulking two stops back. Break into a run again and just as I get there it pulls off. Naturally everyone on the bus acknowledges me except the driver.

I have an hour to wait, in the rain, for the next one. A note on the stop informs me that the bus stops have changed. So the double bus shelter that they put in for the huge Red Arrow queue is now in the wrong place.[177]

One can imagine blogs like these being of inestimable value for future historians. But they bring the private details of people's lives into the public arena, partly by publicising them, and partly by giving them longevity, making them permanent rather than fleeting. They have altered our preconceptions, in the same way that the coffee shops of eighteenth century London helped develop the privatised space described by Habermas.[178]

Many online relationships have this public/private blend. A photograph of some personal aspect of life gets posted on Flickr, and tagged to make it more likely to be found by others during a search. A multiplayer online game might involve very close relationships between virtual avatars. Murder victim Anna Sviddersky became posthumously famous after friends posted an online tribute on MySpace; complete strangers mourned her passing, and grieved.[179] A female blogger, known as 'Abby Lee', who became a celebrity after posting explicit accounts of her energetic sex life, was outraged when her real identity was leaked. 'Who wants their parents reading that stuff? It's private,' she complained.[180] The result is akin to a conversation, but one that is broadcast; privacy here looks more like anonymity. In this ambiguity is the source of many of the issues affecting privacy online.

Some bloggers are much more revealing about their personal lives, and some record their sex lives. Few if any record criminal activities. Many discuss political activism in oppressive countries. Privacy for these people can solely be expressed via anonymity, which, as a number of high-profile cases show, can be broken through the examination of internal evidence, or through someone informing on the blogger. As with any kind of revelation of one's past, blogging is a risk.

With such a rapidly growing community it was not long before trends in the blogosphere became an object of interest. What was being said and the conversations being conducted attracted wide interest, which led to the development of interesting tools and techniques, measurement methods and datasets to try and track the dissemination of an idea or topic through blogspace. Social media analyst Matthew Hurst recently collected link data for six weeks and produced a plot of the most active and interconnected parts of the blogosphere. It contains distinctive regions – for example one region has a preponderance of reciprocal links between blogs, so this is a community where there is much cross citation between each other's postings. A number of blogs are massively popular – the superhubs of the blogosphere. One somewhat isolated group are dedicated blog enthusiasts who use a system called LiveJournal – whilst they are very much in touch with one another they barely connect to the rest of the blogging world.

This form of connected conversational space reflects the interests and issues of the moment. There is a rich space to analyse for those interested in tracing the spread of an idea, the impact of a political initiative, the likely success of a product launch. The much-anticipated release of the Apple iPhone generated 1.4% of all new postings on its launch day. Text analysis tools able to trace the occurrence of key terms featured its rise in sites such as TechMeme and Tailrank which are devoted to the tracking of current themes in the blogosphere. This is yet another area where lots of people are interested in tracking the conversations and interests we have at lots of different scales. We have here a powerful medium for the spread and dissemination of information and varieties of OpEd material. One of the challenges is to understand how this might change our understanding of journalism and media comment. A topic of real concern when sites become large attractors is to determine what mechanisms are there to assure readers that the material and facts quoted adhere to canons of evidence and journalistic quality.

All sorts of issues to do with privacy and security are also raised by the social networking sites, such as MySpace with its 100 million users, Friendster,[181] which manages about thirty million,

Classmates Online,[182] with forty million, and others. From a technical point of view they are a very simple extension to the current Web metaphor. The interesting challenge is what all of these pieces of self-publication and references to other individuals mean in the large. People, often using their real names, post all sorts of information about themselves on social sites. Most of this is harmless, but can include details of friends, activities, blogs read and so on. Sexual orientation and political and religious beliefs often feature too. Young people in particular, whose sense of risk is somewhat smaller, and whose lives are somewhat more party-oriented than their boring elders, can end up giving too much information. Some people have lost jobs or places in college after describing drinking, drug-taking or gay experiences.[183]

WEB 2.0 MEETS THE SEMANTIC WEB

Web 2.0 results in the creation of a great deal of information. An important research issue is how to mine the information that is being collectively published on the Web much more effectively. One example is Wikipedia – widely admired and regarded as a hugely successful Web 2.0 phenomenon comprising high quality user-generated content. In July 2007 it comprised over 1.8 million articles. Wikipedia articles usually consist of free text, but they also contain different types of structured information; categorisation information, images, geo-coordinates, links to external Web pages and, certainly not least, infobox templates (sets of facts about various objects described in Wikipedia). There are about three-quarters of a million English templates with more than 8,000 properties (predicates), with music, animal and plant species, films, cities and books the most prominent types.

With this amount of rich content a number of efforts are underway to release it in a structured fashion on the Web. One of these is DBpedia – DBpedia has harvested the structured data in Wikipedia and produced RDF – effectively a Semantic Web for Wikipedia that one can browse and query. Why is this interesting? Because now our exploration is at a much finer grain size than Web pages – we can query data directly. An application using DBpedia shows how precise our search now becomes: we can ask for all tennis players who live in Moscow, or the names of all the mayors of towns in the US that are at an altitude greater than 1000 metres! We have a very focused type of Semantic Search. Because the underlying representation of information is in RDF the results of such data queries are themselves machine readable, which means that the results can be embedded into existing pages and frameworks or combined with other data in various presentation and visualization frameworks. Imagine the power of this sort of precise query applied to the Web in general – a whole host of facts could become available, such as the aggregation of all of the various sites that refer to individuals, financial affairs, education and health, travel and leisure. The Semantic Web will be another powerful lens through which to view ever increasing amounts of very particular data.

CASE STUDY: MASHUPS

One of the most important Web 2.0 developments is the mashup, an application which brings together data from a number of different sources. For instance, The Profane Game[184] mashes up Google, a Web dictionary and a tool that is meant to detect bad language to create a game where the object is to list as many swear words as possible in 30 seconds. The Wheel of Lunch[185] takes your zip code and tells you where you should eat today. Explore the World Map[186] allows you to click on a map and see YouTube footage shot at that point. safe2pee[187] is a 'community-driven gender-neutral unisex bathroom directory' which makes it possible for the politically correct and desperate to find a unisex public toilet in the city of their choice. Chicago Crime[188] maps a database of reported crimes in Chicago onto a streetplan of that city.

However, not every mashup is so benign. Any two sources of data can be amalgamated, to exploit the power of amalgamated databases. One trend, somewhat disturbing for many people, is to take the data about convicted sex offenders that has to be made available in the United States under Megan's Law, and mash it up with geographical information to create an easy-query environment, to discover who one's friendly neighbourhood sex offenders are. A street map of the district will have the locations of convicted sex offenders pinpointed. Click the mouse on one of the pinpoints, and up come the name, address and criminal record of the sex offender registered as living there. Click on another icon, and up will come the police mugshot. The information is there in milliseconds, and will use the latest registers, so will be up to date and accurate (if the registers are). The value of such a site for concerned parents is obviously great. The value for vigilantes is presumably also not trivial. Note that such sites do not create any extra information, or publish previously secret information. All the information on such sites is in the public domain already. But when it is kept at different locations, on paper, or even in different databases which are relatively hard to search, the effort involved in producing a photograph of your local sex offender would be too high for all but extremely concerned individuals to undertake. Thanks to mashups, this practical obscurity no longer obtains.

Merging data places each item in a new context, which can have all sorts of privacy-reducing effects. The informality of mashups means that information on them need not be reliable, unless someone is willing to go through a long editorial process to ensure its provenance and accuracy. The owner of the data does not know, or care, that the data is being used in this way, while the developer does not own the data and so is generally unable to check its integrity. To take one obvious example, if someone's name accidentally found its way onto the sex offenders' register, or, perhaps more likely, was not removed when it supposedly expired, it would be unlikely that someone running a sex-offender-tracking website would discover the error and correct the site.

In a clever demonstration of the dangers of mashups, consultant Tom Owad mashed up book wishlists published on Amazon with Google Earth, but with a twist. The Amazon users leave a name and a home town, which was often enough to locate them, via Yahoo! People Search, at an individual address, of which Google Earth would hold a detailed satellite image. He also filtered out most of the books, to leave only those who read subversive literature. The result was a map of the world with readers of subversive books located upon it; click on the location of such a reader, and get a high resolution satellite image of his or her house. Of course, Owad was merely demonstrating the principle, not building a usable system for genuine employment by the Thought Police. But ... .[189]

7

THEY SNOOP TO CONQUER: CENSORSHIP, DECISIONAL PRIVACY AND IDEOLOGICAL PRIVACY

We have generally focused in this book on the commonest interpretation of privacy, whereby the subject of information retains control over its distribution. However, other types of privacy feature online. In this chapter we will look at 'decisional privacy', the privacy to make one's own decisions without hindrance, and 'ideological privacy', the privacy to pursue one's own ideas of the good or correct life without being pressured to conform to someone else's ideals. The imposition of national or other standards, thereby impinging on decisional or ideological privacy, is what we call 'censorship'. This is a very live issue online. We will begin by looking at these two types of privacy, before examining how snoopers have migrated onto the Internet.

DECISIONAL PRIVACY

At first blush the ability to make one's own decisions can sound like an odd type of thing to call 'privacy' – it appears to be much more to do with freedom of action than with Warren and Brandeis' right to be let alone. The most famous statement of the right to decisional privacy is, oddly to non-American ears, the Supreme Court judgement of *Roe v Wade*, which established women's rights to abortion in the US.[190] The *Roe* decision argued that anti-abortion laws violated the constitutional right to privacy under the Due Process clause of the Fourteenth Amendment (which is the principle that government must normally respect all of someone's legal rights when they are deprived of life, liberty or property, intended to limit the power of the legal system to transgress basic ideas of justice). A woman was entitled to end a pregnancy, for whatever reason, up until the point at which the foetus becomes viable. The court ruled that, though the state of Texas (whose abortion laws were the subject of the case) had a legitimate interest in preventing or discouraging women from undergoing risky medical procedures, and in preserving prenatal life, those interests did not outweigh the constitutional right of privacy that had been detected in previous Supreme Court judgements in the Fourteenth Amendment and the Due Process clause. Decisional privacy is, in this context, perhaps best seen as another aspect of the retention of control over one's 'inviolable personality'. The decision is my private one and not one that the state has any business regulating.

Decisional privacy certainly impacts online, and there are many examples of the demand for it. For example, in the United States, the online gambling industry is more or less banned.[191] The ability to make private decisions to play poker or bet on horses is highly regulated by most states, and people's rights to privacy are outweighed by the states' interests in such regulation, according to US legal precedent. Online gambling sites have thrived offshore, but the American government has pursued several lines of attack, including preventing banks from processing credit card payments to gambling sites, and arresting gambling executives on racketeering charges when they unwisely stray into American jurisdictions. In Europe, the French government and a number of German states have also acted aggressively towards offshore gambling in order to preserve state gambling monopolies.

In China there are a number of restrictions on online gaming. Multiplayer games such as *World of Warcraft* attract hundreds of thousands, sometimes millions, of players round the world, but the Beijing government is trying to curb such behaviour by restricting players to three hours' gaming at a stretch. In order to stop young people becoming addicted (there have been unsavoury incidents in China as a result of excessive gameplaying, including a murder), players who remain in the game for longer than the maximum can expect to have their in-game characters weakened by the loss of powers or capabilities. Players will have to take a five-hour break before being allowed to play once more.[192] Regulation of the Internet (whether or not justified) once more in this case reduces decisional privacy.

IDEOLOGICAL PRIVACY

Ideological privacy is the ability to hold one's own views without interference. It is generally held in Western democracies that one's religious or political views are one's own affair. However, there are many places where this is not the case; in China membership of many organisations, such as the Falun Gong, is outlawed, for instance. Equally, in the context of the War on Terror, the authorities in democracies are looking aghast at many of the extremist and minority interests which haunt the Internet. In particular, there is a strong nihilistic streak online,[193] and there is a danger that many are able to use the Internet's filtering capabilities to remove contrary opinions, only reading and listening to inflammatory interpretations of the news or culture.[194] From teenage goth nihilists who work themselves up to commit school shootings in America to Islamic neo-fundamentalists,[195] such users of the Internet are dangerous, because their interactions with the world are not through political routes (where alternative and countervailing viewpoints are likely to be encountered), but rather are immediate and violent. In January 2007, for instance, respected Turkish-Armenian journalist Hrant Dink was assassinated by a teenager who believed, mistakenly, that Dink had insulted the Turks, after reading a false report about Dink online.[196]

This issue with freedom of speech is pressing in all forms of communication, but online forums attract those of extreme or non-standard views, partly because the barriers to entry for publishing are so low. It's hard for racists or extreme nihilists to get their views printed in 'respectable' newspapers, or broadcast on the television. The Unabomber Ted Kaczynski had to resort to blackmail to get his manifesto *Industrial Society and its Future* published in the *New York Times* and the *Washington Post* in 1995; the same text is now widely available online.

IDEOLOGIES OF REPRESSION

Ideology plays two roles with respect to online privacy. Ideological privacy is often threatened, but repression is usually justified by ideological arguments. The liberal view that privacy is a necessary support for autonomy, close to being a consensus in many Western democracies, and enshrined in the constitution of the United States, is opposed by various ideologies that do not regard free expression or unhindered freedom of action as being of supreme value. These ideologies of repression are not (all) evil or stupid – they are perfectly reasonable reactions to particular political and social problems, even if ultimately the majority of computer users do not subscribe to them. In particular, they are often embedded in the basic assumptions of particular societies, and Internet liberals need to beware of quasi-imperialism, imposing the freedoms of the Internet on societies that are wary of pornography, gambling or social upheaval. The very name of the World Wide Web self-consciously declares that it is a universal resource for all mankind, but all mankind does not share the ideals of openness and freedom. That may be their loss, but it doesn't alter the fact that the Web can be seen by many as just one more intrusive globalising technology that threatens the basis of particular cultures. We should expect the Web to be both welcomed and resisted.

Before we discuss the actual censorship of the Internet, let's briefly review some features of cultures associated with repressive ideologies that differ from the liberalism enshrined in the American constitution, and prominent in the American tradition, that animates not only the founders and developers of the Internet (most prominently in American universities), but also a large proportion of its user base. We will briefly examine some different non-liberal views on privacy whose roots can be found in different soils: a nationalist take, from China; a pragmatic view, looking at Singapore; a set of ideas with a religious background, looking at the Islamic world; and a recent academic recipe for social harmony.

NATIONAL CULTURE: CHINA

China has benefited from a wide range of social and political theorists, from Taoists to Mohists, Buddhists to Legalists, but perhaps the dominant strain of Chinese thought is Confucianism, a highly social and worldly doctrine which in effect attempts to balance social justice with the realities of an unequal, hierarchical and often cruel society. In a chaotic feudal world, Confucius (551–479BC), and his immediate followers such as Mencius, tried to foster order without resorting to revolutionary schemes that upturn society as a whole.

Chinese philosophy developed along a different route from that of Western Europe, in that the Chinese tended to understand reality as a set of relations, as opposed to Europeans who conceived it as substance.[197] This leads fairly naturally to a focus on discovering identity in *networks* of unique relationships with other objects or beings, as opposed to *sets* of attributes of the object or being itself. The latter, European, way of looking at things makes privacy relatively easy to comprehend – since nothing essential about the object or being in question depends on outside influences, it is straightforward to imagine such influences being cut off. From the Chinese perspective on the other hand, isolating an object or being from its surroundings may well undermine its essential characteristics, by severing key relations with its environment.

As one popular novelist put it, ' "privacy" is a word that is difficult to translate into Chinese. He had stumbled over it several times.'[198] As with Western culture, China developed many variants of the public/private distinction, masked by the use of single words (*gong/si*); for instance, communal interests as opposed to private ones, being public-spirited as opposed to selfish or without authorisation, or being with a witness as opposed to without. In general, privacy contained many negative connotations, while publicity was approved of. Privacy seemed to suggest a secret, clandestine, unsavoury world. On the other hand, the focus of privacy could go beyond the individual, and connote the affairs private to a particular clan based on kinship, in which case private activity, when aimed at promoting the clan, was seen as pleasing ancestral spirits and thereby gaining their blessings.[199] Furthermore, in troubled times when government fragmented, the public sphere did tend to lose some of its lustre and the private sphere conversely appeared more hospitable.[200]

As Chinese society has moved towards a more mainstream development following the death of Mao and the end of the Cultural Revolution, tensions have arisen between reformists, traditional communists and liberals. Liberal attempts to promote free speech and loosen the grip of the Communist Party came to grief in Tiananmen Square in 1989, with the deaths of hundreds, possibly thousands, of demonstrators. Since then, China has pursued reform with a very particular take: economic liberalisation, but little corresponding political liberalisation. This move towards a society with some but not all of the hallmarks of a traditional capitalist society recreated a private space for consumption, which many in China find empty and alienating. That alienation is hinted at, for example, in the ending to Ha Jin's novel *Waiting*,[201] and more explicitly described in Nobel Prizewinner Gao Xingjian's work, for example *One Man's Bible*, where episodes in the oppressive years of the Cultural Revolution are juxtaposed with the unsatisfying freedoms that the West provides.[202]

Pragmatic culture: Singapore

Singapore is vulnerable, a city-state of under 700km² sandwiched between two regional giants, Malaysia (with which Singapore was briefly federated before independence) and Indonesia, with which relations have historically been somewhat hostile. Ethnically, Singapore is mixed, with a population of 76.3% Chinese, 13.8% Malay and 8.3% Indian, mostly Tamil. Securing Singapore's borders against invasion from without, and racial tension within, has been the central policy focus since independence.

It remains democratic, and has frequent and fair elections. However, the People's Action Party (PAP) machine has maintained a ruthless grip on the nation's politics through various legal barriers and sympathetic media, and has won all ten general elections held since independence extremely comfortably (in May 2006, the PAP won 66.6% of the vote, and 82 of the available 84 seats, 37 of which were uncontested). Opposition parties have never achieved more than a handful of MPs. The situation, inconceivable in the West, is accepted because of the PAP's perceived success in delivering security and prosperity (GNP per head in 2003 was US$21,230, about the same as the UK, and several times that of its neighbours).[203]

The vehicle for the provision of security has been economic growth, to secure the legitimacy of the government, reduce racial tension, and provide the funds for effective defence. As a result, much was sacrificed to the goal of effective government. The PAP pursued an open economy and eschewed import substitution, yet still maintained significant levels of control through government-linked companies such as the giant Temasek. It has tried to keep Singaporean industry at the forefront of economic development, most recently by emphasising a 'Knowledge-Based Economy', and it has been able to manipulate the economy by its total control of the legislature and civil service, as well as recruiting from the higher echelons of industry.[204] It is elitist, meritocratic and pragmatic.

The result is, to Western eyes, an odd hybrid. It is a genuine democracy, whose elections are free and fair, and whose government remains accountable (after a particularly bad performance in the 1984 general election, when the PAP received 62.9% of the vote, winning a mere 77 out of 79 seats, some by very small majorities, it made far-reaching changes to its policy platform). It is pretty well free of corruption. But at the same time it is ranked 140th out of 167 in the worldwide Press Freedom index, as the government retains control of expression of public opinion. It is effectively a one-party state; we might call it an illiberal democracy.[205] In the view of the state, privacy can and should be sacrificed to preserve security and prosperity (and, some argue, to preserve the primacy of the PAP as well[206]).

Privacy in Singapore is relatively limited under this paternalistic capitalist system. There is private property, property rights and security in abundance, so private space is well-protected in that sense. On the other hand, behavioural autonomy is suppressed where such autonomy contradicts notions of a desirable society (perhaps most notoriously in the now-repealed ban on chewing gum). And one's opinions are not private: the media and even the

Internet are monitored by the Media Development Authority, and criticism of the PAP has to be measured and careful. Despite being under review since 1992, there is still no government data protection authority.[207]

Religious culture: Islam

If we focus on the example of Islam, we should, of course, beware of assuming a particular determinate class of cultures with a fixed set of properties – the Islamic world stretches from Morocco to Indonesia, and a very large number of Muslims live as minorities in non-Islamic host societies, so variation is large. Nevertheless, for our purposes, it is fair to make a few mild generalisations. There is a distinct value placed on privacy in the Islamic world. The Qur'an says, for instance, that believers' wives are 'as garments to you, as you are to them'[208]. The family unit, in other words, is analogous to one's clothing, a microenvironment which marks off a personal space. But Islamic privacy has a public aspect, and can be created by transforming what to Western eyes would be a public space – perhaps most obviously when a worldly space is converted into a sacred space by marking it and facing Mecca in a ritually pure state during one of the episodes of daily prayer.[209] Many commentators warn against imposing traditional Western concepts and oppositions (public/private, modest/shameless) onto Islamic practices.[210]

Privacy, in much of the Islamic world, is associated with home and family life, and of course in recent years much discussion of the topic has centred on the treatment of women and various practices of veiling, which again creates a mobile and often gendered private space where women are protected from the gaze of male strangers. This has often been seen by feminist commentators as a specific use of privacy as a method of control, of a way for men to marginalise women,[211] although this has been debated. Veiling can also be a method of asserting rank and social status, for instance.[212] And although the claim of one California-based academic that the practice of veiling is actually a strident feminist statement and an expression of resistance to colonial legacies[213] stretches credulity, it is true that veiling is used by young girls to gain the respect of gangs of boys, particularly in poor European neighbourhoods such as the French *banlieues*.[214]

On the other hand, prominent Islamist theorist Tariq Ramadan argues that veiling, though nominally voluntary, can become compulsory *de facto*.

> To offer women the horizon of an inward message of Islam by beginning with the imposition of the veil is tantamount to committing the same reductionism as that which consists of immediately applying a range of sanctions on the social plane without having undertaken the necessary reforms. Repeating at will that Islam asserts that there is "no constraint in religion" does not change the reality of pressure, and *oppression*, that some Muslim women today are subjected to.[215]

In other words, to judge the tradition of veiling as an instance of women's privacy, or women's repression, volition and control are key factors. Banning women from the areas of supermarkets where CDs and DVDs are sold, as happens in Saudi Arabia,[216] is surely less to do with providing privacy and more to do with restricting women's access to potentially immoral pop music or Hollywood films. When a conservative Islamic culture, in which

privacy plays a key role, comes up against the freewheeling World
Wide Web, we should expect friction.

COMMUNITARIANISM

The non-liberal ideologies discussed above have all grown more
or less organically in particular societies – the Singaporean view
being perhaps more top-down than the others. Nevertheless, not
all ideologies emerge from a wider cultural base. Some are developed by pointy-headed folk in universities, and communitarianism is one recent example that has gained some vogue in the
Western world, where selfishness is perceived to be rampant and
social responsibility weak. It is the view that a good society needs
to have in place principles to protect both the common good and
individual rights. The liberal society, in contrast, is seen to privilege
rights, and is therefore, in the communitarian view, unbalanced.[217]

In essence, communitarianism grew up as a reaction against a
perceived growth in the power of individualism, particularly in
the United States. The argument of Warren and Brandeis[218] is
central to the communitarian narrative of America's history as an
independent nation. Up until then (1890), America had been a
country with strong communal values, erring in some areas
(notably racial discrimination) on the side of unjust authoritarian-
ism. The great thinkers of liberalism, Locke, Adam Smith and
Mill, as well as Warren and Brandeis themselves, were attempting
to correct this imbalance, which was perfectly sensible in the
eighteenth and nineteenth century context.

But after Warren and Brandeis' landmark review, which established the right of privacy without limit, independent of all other

rights, the balance shifted. By about 1960, in the communitarian narrative, individual rights had taken precedence. Countercultural expressions of the self, and the celebration of individual autonomy became *de rigueur* in the 60s, to the extent that if one relied on one's culture to provide a moral steer, one was seen as a conformist, or, in the *argot* of the time, a 'square'. The route from individualism to rejection of conformism uses a key concept of John Stuart Mill, that we are all morally rational, and that we can, and should, be able to work out principles of morality for ourselves, rather than taking them on trust.[219] The 1980s continued the rot, promoting unbridled self-interest with a misuse of Adam Smith's market doctrines. The result, by century's end, was a society in which the community was severely wounded, and the individual was king.

Communitarians do not assume privacy is a right. Rather, they view private realms as those in which a person (or group) can legitimately act without disclosure or accountability to others. So privacy requires a social licence, and is a normative idea, as opposed to the simple empirical notion of an absence of surveillance.[220]

Communitarians are not opposed to intrusion into what we might consider our private lives, but they have particular views of what is legitimate and what not. Governmental control is bad, although many communitarians consider fears about the state's encroachment onto our liberties are overdone. Big private institutions actually constitute a bigger threat, taken all in all. But the important brake on destructive individualistic behaviour is the community itself. As Etzioni puts it, 'the best way to curtail the need for governmental control and intrusion is to have somewhat less privacy.'[221]

We earlier described a three-way distinction of public/private realms – the public (state), the private (domestic), and the privatised realm of public opinion. Communitarians recognise a four-way split – in effect, dividing the privatised realm into two. As well as the state and the home, there is the realm of the market, based on individual choices, and there is the community, 'which relies on subtle social fostering of prosocial conduct by such means as communal recognition, approbation and censure. These processes require the scrutiny of some behaviour, not by police or secret agents, but by friends, neighbors, and fellow members of voluntary associations.'[222] This community can indeed be further subdivided into separate social spheres which should not interfere with each other – in other words, one's privacy might be sacrosanct in one context with one set of associates, and open to intrusion in another context with different associates.[223]

CENSORS, SNOOPERS AND HOW TO AVOID THEM

There is a huge culture clash looming in cyberspace. The predominance of American academics in Internet development means that the debate is currently bubbling under the surface, but the growth of other online constituencies means that the arguments will get serious very soon. There have already been important debates over key aspects of Internet governance, for instance with an unsuccessful attempt to wrest control of the Internet Corporation for Assigned Names and Numbers from the United States.[224]

On the side of freedom, there are political liberals, and engineering types who argue that unrestricted flows of information are necessary for the Web to function as successfully as it does. On the side of censorship are political non-liberals, together with people who wish to use offline business models restricting information flow online. Privacy advocates can end up on either side of the divide. Those who see it as a matter of retaining control of information about oneself generally support restrictive measures, while those who wish to see decisional or ideological privacy want to keep information flowing freely.

How is it possible to censor cyberspace? Information moves through the Internet in five phases, each of which can be the location for interference.

1. It begins at the source computer. The person or organisation running that computer is usually legally responsible for the data being distributed, but they can be relatively hard to police as they are often in a different jurisdiction from the destination of the information (where the offence is caused). Tracing the owners of a computer can also be hard.

2. Next the information packets pass through the source's ISP. The ISP, which is usually a *bona fide* commercial outfit, is a correspondingly harder legal target, as it will have access to lawyers and company law to protect its operations. On the other hand, enforcing legal judgements against it is easier than against individuals who could be anywhere in the world.

3. In the third stage, the packets are sent through the Internet in short hops from computer to computer, with different routes for each packet. As the Internet's architecture is meant to make this transfer of data as smooth and effortless as

possible, this is the hardest section of the information's journey to police.

4. The information next arrives at the destination ISP. There is surprisingly little movement to fix legal responsibility on ISPs for content they carry from the Internet.

5. Finally, the information arrives at the destination computer, where it can be censored by the user. Many computers carry filtering software, allowing the owner to remove information that, for instance, they do not want their children or employees to see. The aim of digital rights management (DRM) is to make computers manage content according to publishers' rather than owners' wishes, so that, for instance, one cannot play an illegally downloaded piece of music, although DRM is increasingly unpopular. Tracing people who have downloaded illegal information is very hard, unless they have left some kind of record, such as paying for it with a credit card.[225]

ISPs are usually statutorily required to collect information for the authorities, which is another potential threat to privacy. They also need to collect information about browsing habits in order to ensure freer flow of information, and will possess other information about one's offline life, such as one's home address and credit card details for billing purposes.

One can disguise one's IP address in an interaction by using a *proxy server*, such as anonymouse.org,[226] to route a request for information to the proxy, which is the agent which actually contacts the website. The remote website only needs to know the IP address of the proxy, although of course the proxy needs the original IP address. But if one trusts the proxy to keep the information secure, then the transaction itself is safer. On the other hand, a proxy server certainly possesses a lot of interesting information (the IP addresses of everyone who uses its services, and who therefore wish to be anonymous, as well as all the sites those users have contacted), and of course it is always possible that the proxy itself has been subverted, or is the malicious creation of illiberal authorities.

NATIONAL CENSORSHIP STRATEGIES

The extent to which the Web is censored varies quite dramatically. At one end of the scale, the North Koreans have what is in effect a national Intranet (a private network of computers using Internet protocols) called *Kwangmyong*. A relatively small number of trusted people are allowed access to the Internet, and they harvest interesting content off the Web as a whole and import it into *Kwangmyong*. Hence the risks of an unauthorised North Korean being corrupted are relatively small, although *Kwangmyong* hosts many of the standard services we have come to expect from the Internet, including dating bureaux, email, newsgroups and a search engine. But technology is pushing the boundaries even here; Web-enabled phones may soon allow some North Koreans illicit access to the Web itself via China.[227]

Not that the Chinese Web is entirely free. China is very keen to use the Internet as an economic tool, but does not want to encourage free speech on it. As Internet usage rises (147 million Chinese users as of June 2007[228]), so do the problems for the Chinese authorities, where the Internet is highly policed and regulated by what is called the Great Firewall. This is a multi-faceted approach to preventing the Internet from corrupting the minds of Chinese citizens, while retaining its use as an economic if not a political tool. The Firewall works by using a suite of more or less standard methods of repression: blocking particular IP addresses and domain names, removing information packets if they contain suspicious keywords, and blocking connections.[229] Internet service and content providers are drummed into aiding the censorship.[230] But perhaps the most astonishing statistic is that 30,000 secret policemen are employed to spend their time on the Internet, searching for iffy keywords, trawling through chat-rooms, erasing anti-communist messages and putting forward their own propaganda.[231] Even so, that is about 5,000 users per cop, and the users are also aided by a dazzling array of censorship-avoiding devices.[232] There are tens of millions of bloggers, who are incredibly hard to monitor. The advantages of mobilising China's huge labour force are declining as the Internet grows in size and complexity; the Great Firewall of China will soon be replaced by the Golden Shield, which is a somewhat more hi-tech suite of censorship techniques.[233]

China has a high level of incarceration of online dissidents, caught and monitored through mainly unintelligent techniques.[234] A few dozen activists are in jail, and big corporations have been co-opted into helping the Chinese with their censorship (Google offers a censored version of its search engine, for example). The corporations argue that without them, the Chinese information space would be even more restricted; there is some debate at the moment as to how self-serving an argument that is.[235]

Those who need or want information, and are relatively web-savvy, do manage to find their way around such obstacles;

the result is an arms race between them and the authorities. The censorship of Google, and of the Chinese search engine market leader Baidu, is a relatively simple operation. The user searches for documents containing a keyword in the usual way, but the results of the search are only presented once they have been tested by a firewall which is looking for particular banned addresses, or keywords. So, for instance, one might search for pages containing some innocuous keywords, such as 'psychology', and find a list of pages. But the firewall then checks to see whether they also contain dodgy keywords such as 'Falun Gong', an illegal religious group, for example. So a page which would ordinarily have turned up on a search will not be seen by the user if there are banned keywords on it as well.

This is not an infallible system, because some keywords will always get through the net, as language changes (partly in direct response to the challenges created by the Great Firewall). For instance, during one test, though 'Falun Gong' was filtered out, 'FLG movement' was not.[236] Those with rather more techie credentials also use proxy servers beyond the scope of the Great Firewall. And bloggers, who can make a reasonable guess at what the banned keywords are, can ensure their writings don't contain them (or can disguise banned words with hard-to-find variations, such as 'freeclom', 'libertea' or '\/iagra'). China's control over its Web is not total, therefore; indeed, its failure in 2003 to suppress bad news about SARS from spreading was a major setback for the government (whose partial successes were major setbacks for Chinese citizens' public health). Information about the outbreak spread almost as fast and as virally as the disease itself, via email and messaging services. Similarly, in 2005, a nationalistic campaign against the Japanese, initially fostered by the government for diplomatic purposes, outran its ability to control it, and anti-Japanese sentiment spread over the Internet while the government tried desperately to calm things down.

We should not assume that Internet censorship is always forced on populations by governments. The Saudi government filters various aspects of the Web heavily, focusing on pornography, drugs, gambling and religious conversion, although it has a fairly transparent filtering regime which informs the Web surfer that content has been blocked. When the user receives the message that a page is blocked, there is a link to a form that allows the user to ask to unblock the blocked site, and also – more interestingly – to suggest other sites that should be blocked. According to the Saudi Internet Services Unit (ISU), there are on average 200 suggestions per day of currently unblocked sites to be blocked, and it seems that about 30% of these suggestions are taken up. Although 45% of users found the ISU's blocking too stringent in 1999, 41% were quite happy with it, and 14% thought it too lax. The Saudi authorities feel that these figures demonstrate widespread public support for censorship.[237]

At the other end of the scale, Singapore has a relatively light censorship regime. Thanks to its pursuit of a knowledge economy, there is a high rate of computer literacy, and the value of the Internet in selling ideas rather than commodities is of course vast. But, like China, the Singaporean authorities worry about the potential evil influences of the Internet, not so much to exercise political control and perpetuate the one party state (although that may well be a motive), but because of the premium Singapore places on social cohesion.

Nevertheless, the Singaporean government recognises the great efforts required to patrol cyberspace. Hence its main strategy is to single out particularly bad sites and focus on them. A number of pornographic sites are banned. Political and religious websites have to be registered as content providers with the Singapore Broadcasting Authority, and since 2001 there should be no online campaigning during election campaigns by non-political sites, no polling or election surveys, and no appealing for funding.[238] In an empirical test, the OpenNet Initiative, a campaigning organisation for free speech online, found that relatively few sites were blocked (under half of one per cent of their sample of potentially offensive sites).[239] In general, with a small political class, the People's Action Party government can exercise a good deal of information control simply by its licensing activities, and by threats of defamation suits.

All in all, of these models, the Chinese one is particularly pernicious, as its monitoring is opaque; when you fail to download bbc.co.uk or wikipedia, you do not know whether the connection has simply timed out, or alternatively whether it has been blocked. In Saudi Arabia, you are warned that you have tried to access a banned page. Singapore does not interfere with the Web directly very much, and prefers to use heavy-handed legal sanctions. The number of North Korean users is too small to be particularly significant. But China is a major player on the Internet – one user in eight is Chinese, a fraction exceeded only by that of Americans. Not only that, at the moment only one tenth of the Chinese population is connected to the Internet, so further growth is inevitable, and it is only a matter of time before China overtakes America in Internet usage.

Surveillance

Censorship is one aspect of the infringement of online privacy; another is active snooping. Indeed, from the earliest days of computing it was clear that unwanted intrusion was going to figure large. One could say that the very earliest computers invaded privacy – but in one nation's interest. The machines conceived and built by the British in the Second World War had one purpose. They existed to decrypt the encrypted signals of the German Military-Industrial complex. The first machines to decrypt the Enigma machine – the multi-rotor cipher machines used by the Germans – were in fact analogue electro-mechanical devices. Nevertheless these remarkable machines, so-called Bombes, were the product of Alan Turing and Gordon Welchman's genius. They could each simulate 36 Enigma machines and by using 300 Bombes the British had usually broken the more important of the Germans' daily codes before breakfast.[240]

When the Germans introduced much more complex cipher machines, another remarkable device was designed – the Colossus. This machine had much more of the electronic computer about it, using punch tape, valves and a whole array of innovative techniques to search a huge space of possible encodings. Both Colossus and the Bombe were kept secret and destroyed after the War. But they showed the remarkable power that electronic information processing could deliver. It is estimated that they shortened the war by up to two years.[241]

Of course the ability of State and National Security Agencies to spy on their own and other nationals is well appreciated, and although a cloak of secrecy necessarily hangs over much of this work, basic facts are a matter of public record. For instance, the US National Security Agency (NSA) created a global spy system codenamed ECHELON which intercepts huge numbers of communications – phone, fax and email – sent anywhere in the world. ECHELON, although controlled by the NSA, is operated in conjunction with GCHQ in the UK and analogous agencies in Australia, Canada and New Zealand. This arrangement harks back to relations established during WWII.

ECHELON intercepts are processed using a variety of state-of-the-art data mining and pattern recognition systems as well as the intelligence of large numbers of analysts. The ECHELON components are primed to look for code words or phrases (known as the ECHELON 'Dictionary'). Intelligence analysts at each of the respective 'listening stations' maintain separate keyword lists for them to analyze any conversation or document flagged by the system, which is then forwarded to the respective intelligence agency headquarters that requested the intercept.[242]

The CIA in the US has famously run operations against its own citizens. Investigations of Operation Chaos revealed that the CIA had compiled files on thousands of individuals, including US citizens and several domestic organizations. The *New York Times* reported that, while conducting Operation Chaos, 'The agency compiled a computer index of 300,000 names of American people and organizations, and extensive files on 7,200 citizens.'[243]

The Internet is a gift for organised crime and international terrorism; terrorist groups in particular, with their loose network structures, find cyberspace a very congenial home. They use the Internet and the Web: to put over their particular narratives of conflict, which would otherwise not get an airing over state-influenced media; to release communiqués and speeches; to radicalise young people and children with computer games and simplified stories; to pass messages and issue orders anonymously between operatives; to mine data about potential terror targets; to recruit new members; to indoctrinate interested parties; to disseminate instructions and online manuals, such as *The Mujahadeen Poisons Handbook*, *The Anarchist's Cookbook* or al-Qaeda's online training manual *Al Battar*; to plan missions; to raise funds; and to conduct ideological debates or arguments with rival terror organisations.[244]

Given all that, it is unsurprising that the authorities have actively sought ways of intercepting communications. Shortly after the attacks of 11 September 2001, President Bush signed into law a piece of legislation with one of those toe-curling American names, the Uniting and Strengthening America by Providing Appropriate Tools Required to Intercept and Obstruct Terrorism Act (USA PATRIOT Act, geddit?) which increased the surveillance capabilities of law enforcement and intelligence agencies, and supported the (already legal) monitoring of emails and other traffic. Emails, for instance, can be intercepted, and interrogated at various levels of specificity and intrusion. An email contains all sorts of information in addition to the message itself. When intercepted, depending on what is authorised, law enforcement agents might just look at the email header, which will tell them who is contacting whom, but not what about, or with stronger authorisation could look at the message itself or its attachments.

The controversial Carnivore system (now renamed DCS1000 to make it sound less scary)[245] is used by the FBI to 'sniff out' Internet traffic, working somewhat like a wiretap. As packets of information are sent around the Internet, Carnivore intercepts them and inspects them. It can record all of the email messages sent to or from a particular email account, or all of the network traffic to or from a particular IP address, the webpages down-loaded to a particular IP address, or track everyone who accesses a particular page. It is a passive system that does not change mes-sages or prevent anyone from getting any information, and is used on the basis of court order. Its information-processing capabili-ties, however, are not infinite. Legislative oversight of the system is not perfect, but it is unrealistic to expect email traffic not to be monitored in these troubled times. Nevertheless, the lack of seri-ous auditing of the use of the system, and indeed all surveillance systems in the fevered post-September 11 atmosphere, remains a problem.[246]

The Internet is a privatised space, with public and private aspects, of the sort that have been described by thinkers such as Arendt and Habermas. In one sense, as the Carnivore example proves, it is as public as the public highway, in that the headers of the information packets that get passed around contain reference to the IP address of the recipient. So information routes can be tracked, and though encryption can hide the *contents* of the pack-ets, it does not hide the *destination*. As noted above, one way around this is to use a proxy server, although whoever runs the proxy server has access to all the IP addresses of those who use its services – which is a pretty devastating piece of information if the proxy is a front for a government or a wrongdoer, or the target of hacking. More complex methods of disguising the IP address, such as using networks of proxies (so-called *onion routing*), are correspondingly more complex to interact with.

The authorities, of course, fight back, and when they spot a proxy, they block access to it exactly as they would block access to any other website. But the community of Internet users is pretty nimble, and lists of non-blocked proxies pass around freely, via email, blogs or instant messaging. There is even software available that automatically finds proxies from a constantly updated list; Tor[247], for instance, is a network of 'virtual tunnels', in effect distributing your transactions across several places all over the Internet, thereby making it much more difficult for you to be tracked down. Each proxy will stand until it is discovered, which may take a while; the giant labour force available to China's censors works quickly, but even so may take some days to find a proxy. The quieter the proxy, the longer, generally speaking, it will last.[248]

CASE STUDY: 'SOUSVEILLANCE'

The model which we have implicitly adopted is one of watchers putting us under surveillance, and our attempting to evade their view. But the technologies available to the watchers are staggering. If we stick to this view of privacy, then we are finished before we even start. We cannot possibly keep track of what The Powers That Be are doing to us, because there are simply too many opportunities to view our behaviour. Tracing the use of information about us will be a Herculean task of which none of us is capable, even those of us obsessed about the whole issue.

Legal guidelines are of little help. For instance, the standard OECD guidelines of 1980 predate the period of major expansion of the Internet, but were revisited in 1998 by an OECD ministerial committee, and judged still sound in the new context. Nevertheless, some commentators, notably security and privacy consultant Roger Clarke in an extensive paper,[249] have argued that the privacy protection supported by the guidelines is inadequate, as they focus more firmly on the protection of dataflows across borders. The guidelines mitigate harms to governments and corporations, not individuals.

In a novel twist to the privacy debate, science fiction writer David Brin argues that the apparent trap in which we find ourselves is a result of our looking at the problem the wrong way round. Preserving privacy, on the traditional view, involves building defensible cyber-walls around ourselves. But where is this knowledge about information use to come from? Brin's suggestion is that the obvious way to gain transparency is to use the very surveillance techniques that are being used on us. To Juvenal's famous question '*Sed quis custodiet ipsos custodes?*' (but who guards the guardians?), the answer is: we do.

Brin's idea is that information should be as easily available as feasible, consistent with fair payment, protection for intellectual property and so on. Surveillance information is powerful because access to it is monopolised by a few and denied to the rest of us. The more we can all see, the less chance anyone gets the particular power associated with exclusive knowledge. This inversion of the status quo has been called *sousveillance.*[250]

For example, if there is a CCTV camera set up in a particular area, why not broadcast the shots on the Internet, rather than simply relaying them to a security guard or the police? The cameras are more or less inevitable, but the fundamental question is who controls them? This sounds, to many, like a cop out, and a situation even worse than we might first have thought. Instead of one policeman seeing one picking one's nose in the car park, possibly hundreds of people will. The exposure seems dramatically greater. But Brin denies that this will necessarily threaten our privacy – a value he is keen to preserve. He argues that openness gives some measure of protection of the weak from the powerful. As things stand, the protection of privacy is a rich person's game. Those with the resources and the understanding of technology are able to employ advisors, or to buy privacy-enhancing gadgets, whereas the rest of us are open to being watched at any time. Sousveillance levels the playing field. The danger with surveillance technology is not that it is used by too many people, but that it is used by too few. Furthermore, in most arguments on the topic, there is a tacit assumption that privacy is for me, while transparency is for you. For Brin this is a double standard. Openness, transparency, should be reciprocal.

It could be a recipe for alienation or atomisation of society, but Brin does not accept that privacy and liberty are incompatible – indeed far from it. He holds that freedom is extremely important, and would choose liberty, even if a dangerous liberty, every time if the alternative was a 'coddled tyranny'. But he argues that this is a false dichotomy: a free and knowing people should be able to claim and enforce a little privacy, so privacy is a by-product of freedom.

The sousveillance concept shares a number of assumptions with mainstream liberalism, in particular the values of freedom, transparency and accountability, but denies the claim that impeding the flow of information will necessarily promote privacy. In a free society, we should be able to defend privacy via the power to hold accountable those who violate it. A warier liberal response argues that individual autonomy will be threatened by sousveillance in exactly the same way as it is threatened by surveillance. It doesn't matter if the watcher is one very powerful person or a group of less powerful ones. As John Stuart Mill argued, the 'soft power' of public disapproval of one's behaviour can be very restrictive, unfair – and unaccountable – indeed.[251]

8

WHERE DUST IS SMART AND REALITY MIXED: PERVASIVE COMPUTING

INTELLIGENT SPACES

The two main paradigms of computing are very straightforward. In the domestic setting, a big white box sits in the spare room, together with a grubby monitor screen. Mum and Dad use it for shopping, banking and writing up the parish newsletter, while the kids disappear in there for hours on end for reasons that may or may not be innocent. Granny has always wondered why someone has tied a typewriter to a television. It is a separate, and separable, component of family life.

At work, it is an indispensable tool. A PC sits on each office worker's desk, acting as information store, interactive diary, reminder system, stationery store and communication system. Even manual workers need the computer, to work out their schedules, order spare parts or prepare invoices. The computer is a gatekeeper – or a convenient scapegoat – as immortalised in a running joke in the sketch show *Little Britain*, where every week, Carol, on being asked a question, randomly types on the keyboard for a while before intoning 'Computer says no'.

But other paradigms are appearing. Information technology is becoming smaller, and more interlinked; to the naked eye it is disappearing. The technology becomes embedded in physical objects, and the spaces in which we live and work.[252] Our cars are currently closest to this vision, but embedded computing is increasingly frequently encountered. Indeed, as Payne and MacDonald point out, the 170 million PCs shipped in 2004 account for under 2% of the number of processors sold in that year; the other 98-odd% were embedded in mobile phones, TVs, washing machines and so on.[253] The technology integrated into such devices provides information and support in a contextually-relevant but non-intrusive way, ideally improving our lives, making us more efficient, and augmenting our experience of the physical world. Put another way, the physical and the digital world blur into each other. Once more, this is not science fiction. Pervasive systems are with us now – for instance, you can now buy Nike running shoes with sensors that can talk to an Apple iPod, so that the iPod plays music that is in time with your running rhythms, and gives you feedback on your exercise.[254] Rentokil has produced a mousetrap that alerts maintenance staff when it catches something.[255]

There are wonderful opportunities with embedded, pervasive technologies. Furthermore, research programmes are well under-way, and they will ultimately deliver. No doubt the hype is excessive. The South Korean city of Songdo, also known as 'Ubiquitous City', is a giant property development where everything in the environment will be connected – for future business models that have not yet emerged[256] (i.e. the idea of a totally wired city is cool but it's not obvious it will have anything to do). But we need to be mindful of risks: computers and sensors all around us may be able to monitor us, and yet we may be unaware of their presence.

There are four key principles of pervasive computing, as described by Uwe Hansmann et al,[257] of which the first is *decentralisation*. When computing first took off, powerful mainframe computers would do all the work, and pass the results to stupid terminals. Pervasive computing reverses this idea entirely. In this paradigm, all the computing is done by basic, small devices that do specific tasks relatively unintelligently, and communicate to other devices in an open community whose structure of connections changes dynamically. If there is central control, it is only at the level of the queries asked, or demands made, of the system as a whole by (usually human) users.

The second principle is that of *diversification*. Rather than a single type of device, a universal computer that can do pretty well any computationally-feasible task, pervasive devices are small and special-purpose, supplying just a few, or even one, type of information, and need not necessarily work as well, or at all, outside the intended environment.

The third principle is *connectivity*. The key to getting dumb machines to produce powerful and intelligent behaviour is to connect them and let them send their information to other devices that want it and can use it. The system will typically consist of several different devices in parallel, linked by an underlying infrastructure. The Internet will often be important here, and in particular the wireless Internet which allows flexible positioning of sensors without the hard and fast location requirements of fixed lines. But it is not required – devices can be connected simply by using a local area network (LAN), if there is no need for wider connectivity.

And the fourth principle is *simplicity*, not just the simplicity of the devices, but of our interactions with them. Computing can only become pervasive if we don't notice it is there. If we constantly have to readjust systems, enter data, switch things off and on again, or manage their connections, then they will not become pervasive because they will be impossible to forget or ignore. Similarly, open standards are important. At the moment, there are few standards or protocols (analogous to the protocols that enable the Web to work) governing connections between small devices. Standards are certainly necessary, to make it easier to build networks (currently, each pervasive network needs to be constructed by hand), but equally the standards need to be open to be as non-restrictive as possible.

Sensors and hardware

Having an understanding of the physical environment depends on the quality and quantity of the sensors available. The power that Moore's Law bequeaths means that it should be possible to surround ourselves with tools capable of gleaning a very rich diet of data. And sensing and computing should go on in the background, so we need give them no thought whatsoever. We very rarely have cause to think about the computing that goes on while we drive today's cars, for example. That seamlessness sets a number of requirements for pervasive technologies to be genuinely unobtrusive.

Power requirements need to be low; not only does one not want a huge panoply of batteries and wires, but also it would be hard to forget a technology for which there is a large maintenance and power bill to pay every month. Memory needs to be capacious and accurate, and of course the greater the storage capacity the more information can be stored, and therefore gathering the same quantity of information requires fewer read-and-delete sessions. Ideally as much information as possible should be transmitted wirelessly. The sensors need to be robust enough to live in potentially hostile industrial, urban or natural conditions. Finally, interfaces for the hardware need to be uncomplicated, and where the devices interact directly with humans, the display of information needs to be integrable with normal workflow or behaviour patterns, perhaps requiring small, mobile or even flexible display screens.[258]

Passing information from device to device is important. For instance, 'near-field communication' (NFC), developed by Sony and NXP, is a wireless technology that works only at extremely short distances, and is aimed primarily at the mobile phone market. Two devices establish contact (a 'handshake') using NFC only when they are very close to each other indeed. A mobile or a smart card with NFC technology means it can be swiped close to a reader which will allow a very small exchange of data between the two devices, ideal for a financial transaction. Despite the popularity of credit and debit cards, cash is still king for small transactions, but NFC is cheap enough to undercut the costs of banking cash. Prepayment systems mean that the transaction would be relatively low-risk for the merchant, while the purchaser's losses are limited in the event of the phone or card being stolen, as with cash.[259]

Sensor size is plummeting. Indeed, so small are some sensors that they are known as 'smart dust'.[260] A piece of smart dust (called a 'mote') is an autonomous computer with a volume of around one cubic millimetre capable of sensing and communicating information wirelessly. Clustered together, many motes would be able to create flexible and powerful networks of sensors.

Smart dust sounds a bit sci-fi, but similar ideas are already off the drawing board – the case study about RFID tags at the end of this chapter shows that pervasive computing is very much in the here and now. Plastic smart cards with an embedded microchip which can store information and transmit it to a reader are somewhat safer and more private than older cards with a magnetic strip, being both more flexible and better at preventing information being read by unauthorised readers. Perhaps their most common use is to store identifying data that authorises people to enter or leave buildings or rooms, but they can be used for any information-based transactions, including being used as methods of payment, and allowing travel on public transport. Personal digital assistants (PDAs) allow people to carry out computing tasks on the move, they are small enough to hold in the hand, or slip into a jacket pocket or handbag, and are able to connect to the Internet when they find a suitable signal. Such devices can either be seen as extensions of standard computing (and appear with Windows operating systems), or can focus on more novel applications. And mobile phones and computers are converging all the time, with the success of the BlackBerry, Research In Motion's wireless email device, showing how the right portable application with the right interface can sweep at least some portions of the world.

THE PROMISE OF PERVASIVE COMPUTING: SURVEILLANCE, INFORMATION AND MIXED REALITY

Pervasive computing systems can be used to develop intelligent spaces with three essential components. In the first place, there needs to be some kind of space where people or objects interact. This is usually physical, a home, a business, or a road system where cars need to be managed. But it could be virtual, such as an online role-playing game for multiple players. Or it may be a physical space with no serious human involvement, pristine environments where human activity would be deleterious, or hostile environments where it could be dangerous, but where it is important to know how the environment is evolving.[261] Secondly, there needs to be some kind of digital infrastructure that can reason about the space and provide services. And thirdly, there needs to be an interface between the physical and the digital, where small, high performance, low cost devices embedded in the space can send information. There may also be a set of further devices to feed advice or instructions back to users or into the environment, or to change the environment in some way.

Pervasive computing works particularly well in three kinds of task. First, more thoroughgoing and intelligent monitoring of the physical world can lead to greater efficiency, a better interaction, or a greater understanding. The system itself can be improved by the technology. Understanding more about the use of a building can help make it greener; heating systems can be turned off, or adjusted to the number of people inside. Understanding more about patterns of sales of goods can make transportation more efficient. Understanding more about cars using the roads can help reduce congestion. Constant monitoring of soil moisture can help make irrigation systems more targeted and less wasteful.

As far as surveillance systems go, there are all sorts of viable home-based applications. Imagine an alarm system that used sensors to detect movement in a house, or the breaking of door or window circuits, and then some kind of actuator that initiated a security protocol, such as notifying the police, sending the occupant of the house a text message, or sounding an alarm (or all three). Imagine heating systems that could detect temperature and room occupancy and work as intelligent thermostats. Imagine white goods that could diagnose faults, or at least gather information about their own functioning, send the information to an engineer back at head office (not necessarily even in the same country), and alert the owner, so that the engineer can arrive carrying the spare parts that may be required, even before the appliance has actually malfunctioned. Imagine refrigerators that can alert their owners when food they are storing is approaching its sell-by date. Imagine electricity and gas meters that read themselves and send the reading directly to the power company. Indeed, an energy application could bill us on the basis of weekly, daily or even hourly use (it could even take money directly from a named bank account, and not bother us with the bill). It is not out of the question that it could buy electricity from different suppliers at different times of the day, if one company offered a better rate during the night and another a better peak time rate. And, finally, remember the spy in the coffee machine – systems that monitor health could easily be embedded into the home. One's jewellery could monitor vital signs and send data to remote processing computers. None of these applications is technologically unfeasible, and some are already in use.

Monitoring the environment is also a key research area. For instance, cheap sensors are helping produce huge quantities of data for pollution monitoring. Typically, pollution is monitored by special-purpose stations placed at strategic intervals across cities, states or countries, but they are expensive and of course fixed. But put small pollution sensors together with a GPS receiver and a data recorder into a cyclist's backpack and a huge amount of data can be created about pollution at different times of the day and different locations; the cyclist's trips need not be especially for the purpose of gathering information, but rather the information could be gathered as a by-product of normal usage of the bicycle. One project has even monitored air pollution using sensors and GPS receivers fitted to pigeons.[262]

The second type of task for which pervasive computing is well-suited is the provision of extra information to augment a user's experience of the physical world. So, for example, in a museum visitors might be able to download information about the exhibits, or their creators, or their social and historical context. Or the combination of GPS system and petrol gauge could direct a driver to the nearest petrol station when the tank is low, or even interact with the various automated driving systems to ensure that the car maximises its use of petrol when the tank is nearly empty. In this kind of area, it is the individual who benefits rather than the system as a whole.

Travel is an important focus for pervasive computing of the second type – after all, many of us have access to information through books, television or the Internet while at home, whereas on the move one is remote from traditional information sources. And information is often what one needs while travelling – traffic conditions, connecting trains, navigation, communications, even games to play and music to listen to. A high-tech tourist information system could send descriptions of landmarks to one's phone or PDA as one walks near them. Commercial transport is also very information-heavy – the logistics business sends goods around the world with tiny cost margins, and information is crucial for real-time fine-tuning of route planning, maintenance of fuel stocks and pick-up plans.[263] But, as we have seen in other contexts, information gathered by a ubiquitous transport system can also be a force for control and surveillance. Toyota, for instance, is planning a car to prevent drunk driving. Sensors in the steering wheel detect the level of alcohol in the driver's sweat; a dashboard camera senses dilated pupils; onboard computer systems spot erratic steering. If these systems decide the driver of the vehicle is smashed, off goes the engine.[264]

In the commercial context, something that understands one's behavioural profile (for example using information from loyalty cards) could send personalised, targeted advertisements – or even trigger advertisements from retailers in one's vicinity while one is on the move (this is something that one would have to opt into, if it was not to become tedious and disruptive). Checking out of a supermarket may become obsolete – RFID tags and smart payment cards, together with a reader able to link the information together and some biometric security, might mean one could merrily wheel one's trolley out of the supermarket without either queueing or being arrested.[265]

The third type of pervasive system is the mixed reality environment, which perhaps needs a little bit more imagination and description. Such environments are really intended to bring physicality into the digital world, and information and intelligence into the real one. Hybrid spaces might be relatively trivial or deadly serious. As an example of the former, consider the world of gaming. There is already a good deal of interest in games held in persistent online environments, created by a company and populated by gamers' avatars, such as *Second Life* and *World of Warcraft*.[266] Pervasive computing allows the environment to move partly offline, and players can be real, not avatars.

For instance, in the British game *Uncle Roy All Around You*,[267] developed in 2003 by interactive mixed reality artistic collective Blast Theory, the Mixed Reality Lab at the University of Nottingham and British Telecom's Radical Multimedia Lab, participants have to find 'Uncle Roy'. Players come in two types. Online players are dropped into a virtual city, and are tasked with trying to find postcards hidden somewhere on the streets of a real city. Street players, with handheld computers, navigate the real city following the instructions of Uncle Roy. Via their computers, they can see the progress of the online players in their virtual version of the real city; similarly, the online players can see where the street players are, and can communicate with them to direct them to the postcards they are trying to find (only a street player can discover the real postcards in a real city). Real actors in the city serve to confuse the situation. The result has been called an 'hour of paranoia', where remote players become bound to each other with links of trust, and a new form of theatre could be discerned where the moral challenge of mainstream drama boiled down to personal one-to-one experiences, and the interactive gaming experience was imbued with 'questions and riddles that a game or a DJ would never dream of posing'.[268]

A more serious example of mixed-reality can be found in increasingly information-thirsty military operations. In the sort of densely packed urban environments that host many twenty-first century conflicts, terrains can be extremely hostile. Guerrilla forces, terrorists or organised criminal gangs who have grown up in those environments know them inside out, can often rely on shelter from sympathetic locals, and also have the ability to identify, punish and therefore deter informants. Conventional military forces have two major advantages over such opposition, but the first, efficient and overwhelming firepower, is useless in such environments unless large numbers of civilian casualties are contemplated. Furthermore, many of the missions which take place in urban environments are peacekeeping missions, where offensive firepower would be inappropriate to say the least.

So the second advantage, technology, becomes crucial. Soldiers' perceptions of their environment need to be augmented by information in real time, and such augmentation needs to be completely straightforward; a soldier should not have to consult a PDA constantly, for instance, while remaining vigilant about potential visible threats. There is a military imperative to provide centrally-collected information to soldiers, and allow them to gather information and share it with their colleagues without effort on their part. One ambitious gadget is a helmet whose visor provides a transparent display mapped onto the view through it, showing street and landmark names, indicating what is round the next corner, even identifying threats such as sniper positions established by reconnaissance.[269]

Current research into the US's 'Future Force Warrior' programme (FFW) envisages deployment of the technology beginning in 2010. Individually, the technologies that soldiers use, such as night vision systems or satellite positioning units, work well, but integration is missing. So the FFW programme is intended to create a single information system where many of the nodes are individual soldiers. Their uniforms will include smart threads next to the skin to monitor vital signs, to determine not only the soldier's fitness and stress levels, but also, in the event of wounding, to get some idea of the extent of injuries so that medical teams can be alerted immediately, know exactly where to go, and are prepared for the first aid they will have to apply. The uniforms will also be armoured, and fitted with power generators for the sensors, cooling and heating systems for extreme environments, and so on. The soldiers' helmets will project an image inside the visor presenting information. As the technology improves, then so will the marriage between human and technology; future innovations are likely to be improved communication from the helmets, with sharper displays, and the possibility of even showing real time video from elsewhere in the battlefield, and armour enhanced by hydraulic systems to give soldiers superhuman strength.[270]

The technologies being used to build such systems now are not beyond current capabilities. They include geographical information systems that create an accurate duplicate of the real-world space by integrating data from maps, satellite imagery, aerial photography and so on. The virtual space could be enhanced with metadata about the identifiable features (for instance, key locations such as energy or telecommunications installations might be noted). Tracking software could determine the location of the viewer, perhaps from GPS coordinates and comparison with real-world video imagery, thereby ensuring that the presentation of the virtual analogue of the real-world space is presented to the user appropriately. Information provisioning systems could filter superfluous information out of the user's displays, and ensure that the appropriate information is available when needed. And finally, interfaces could enable the user to interact with the wider system. These might include cameras and sensors to relay information about the offline environment back to the online system, sensors and microphones to relay information about the soldier to the online system, and displays and headsets to relay information to the soldier.[271]

PRIVACY IN THE PERVASIVE WORLD

The three types of world mediated by pervasive computing all have different privacy issues involved with them, but in each case the switch from offline to online creates new problems. Invasion of offline privacy requires a physical presence. But once a world migrates online, remote surveillance becomes possible. Obviously getting sensors in place (such as the spy in the coffee machine) requires physical action, which could be done either with or without the knowledge and cooperation of the resident. But once the information from the coffee machine is being passed to a third party, the possibilities mushroom. A surveillance system can be used to gather information that can be potentially very damaging to privacy for obvious reasons. An information-providing system can undermine privacy by helping observers understand what information one is after. For example, if retailers were able to hack into a travel information system (such as a simple satnav system with access to a database of points of interest), they could intercept a query about nearby petrol stations and respond with directions to a particular station (possibly further away and on a less convenient route). A more sinister piece of hacking could discover where one was intending to drive. In a mixed reality system, the dangers of an enemy hacking into an online battlefield, discovering an army's plans and the state of its information, and maybe even feeding misinformation into the system, are manifold and manifest.

But ensuring privacy in pervasive systems is not trivial. Ordinarily, cryptography is the method tailored to ensure security and privacy. Information is encrypted into a form whereby it cannot be easily read or altered by eavesdroppers, and this approach is of course important in the pervasive computing world as it is in other digital areas.[272] But there is an extra problem in the pervasive world, which is that the devices that make up a pervasive system are of necessity small and cheap, and their design will not incorporate the capacity for heavy-duty computing power. This entails that any encryption that they do will be relatively simple, and easily breakable using brute force by larger, more powerful devices. In addition, the devices in pervasive systems generally use wireless communication technology – meaning that there are no wires requiring a physical intervention to allow eavesdropping. Anyone can intercept the radio transmission.

Pervasive computing consists of large networks of interlinked heterogeneous devices. Ideally, one should not try to limit the scope by limiting the devices that can be attached to the network – if it makes sense to place a device in the coffee machine and throw the information gleaned from that into the general mix, then that ought to be possible. This means that standards for communication between devices over the network need to be open, and not too prescriptive; they should not rule things out. But complex security measures are precisely the sort of obstacle to seamless communication between heterogeneous devices that will make some types of communication difficult and others impossible. If the pervasive system is really to melt into the background, then we don't want to be messing around with passwords, or deciding that only certain devices can be connected to other devices. Privacy protection currently tends to work with a defined set of partners and parameters, but the decentralisation implied by the ubiquitous world means that many things must be undefined, and the system must cope with arbitrary connections. Verifying data, transferring consent to access information, auditing interactions must all take place without any central authority being responsible. Decentralisation improves communications, but as with the Web, makes it all the more difficult to keep tabs on all the interactions.[273]

Relatedly, the system is a network of devices, and so can be compromised by very minimal interventions. If a malicious eavesdropper could gain control of a small number of the nodes in the network (maybe even a single device), then it could be possible to attack the network as a whole. This means that the network is very vulnerable. It also means that there are as many points of attack as there are nodes in the network – every device must be made attack-resistant (expensively) to ensure the security of the system.

The systemic nature of a pervasive system raises a number of important questions about interfacing. When one is dealing with a PC, or a standard application (for example, the writing of this chapter using Microsoft's Word software), then there is a central entity with which one interacts. The keyboard is pressed, the new characters appear in the document, the document itself is shown on the screen, saved, backed-up and so on, all through the medium of the window in which the document appears, run by Word. Interaction between Word and the author or reader of the document is straightforward. With a pervasive system, this isn't the case. There is no central computer or piece of software with which one interacts – this, once more, is the point of computing that recedes into the background so that the user doesn't notice it is there. But if one does not interact with the system in a 'normal' way, then how does one monitor its operation? How does one know what data it is collecting, where the data is going, or what happens when one makes some sort of adjustment to the system? As Soppera and Burbridge put it, 'the lack of a clear user interface introduces a tension between technology and human factors'.[274]

Very ambitious pervasive networks are still on the drawing board, and many experiments are underway. There is nothing outlandish about the technology, and no reason to believe that the sorts of system being discussed here will not come into being, but the privacy concerns at the moment are minimal. Some technologies, such as the iPot discussed in chapter one, are already in place for early adopters but highly pervasive networks are still very experimental. Mixed reality environments such as *Uncle Roy All Around You* are currently the prerogative of experimental theatre groups and publicly-funded research projects. Genuinely pervasive systems tend to be deployed in highly restricted environments, such as the GlacsWeb project which monitors changes in glaciers;[275] as Soppera and Burbridge point out ironically, 'measuring humidity in a forest is unlikely to cause any great privacy uproar.'[276]

There is a lot of work currently supporting the development of privacy enhancing protocols, such as P3P, the World Wide Web Consortium's Policy for Privacy Preference (see chapter 3), but this kind of policy-aware computing is unlikely to be the whole of the answer for the pervasive world. The nature of pervasive systems means that there is no 'central locus' of the computing events that would be able to present a top-down view of the privacy policy of the system as a whole, while the complexity of expressing, negotiating and policing a typical privacy policy will swamp the lightweight resources of the individual devices in a pervasive network. One way of dealing with this is to ensure that data from sensors or other devices is only ever sent out with information about how it was gathered, so its provenance is encoded directly into the data. But there are complex research issues still to be addressed. In pervasive systems, data may have multiple owners or interested parties (how many people might we expect to see in a day's images from a CCTV camera?), and if all those owners negotiated separately about the use of the information the result would be highly complex and in practice would prevent the information from being used at all.[277] It is certainly not obvious whether it will be possible to split data up to meet such situations, nor even whether data that has been split up will be useful.

Furthermore, a pervasive network interacts with people in an *ad hoc* way that varies with context. A CCTV camera might capture images of a series of people, but is unlikely to have the resources to determine who those people are or identify them online. And if it did – for example, using face recognition software – that might actually aggravate privacy concerns rather than alleviate them. A Privacy Awareness System suggested by Langheinrich might help in some respects; the system he envisages involves sensors broadcasting their identity to the environment, so that people can detect the signal with their own privacy-protecting devices and use it to trace a piece of software associated with the sensor (but not run by or stored in the sensor) which will negotiate privacy settings.[278] The main point of such a system is that the working out of the privacy issues would not actually have to be done by the network devices themselves.

Working out what the social and technical issues actually are is still a matter for research. Many pervasive computing devices may be attached to a person, either voluntarily (as with the pollution monitors on bicycles), passively (as with mobile phones) or unknowingly (as with some RFID tags); if such devices have location detectors, many other things might be inferred about a person. Controlling the release of such knowledge can be very hard, and methods can be divided roughly into two categories. Policies, agreements, permissions and a legal framework work well when the monitoring of location is consensual, and no-one is acting in bad faith. But when there is lack of consent or bad faith, there have to be methods for reducing, encoding or mangling the positional information that one is sending out.[279] Even getting the right technical languages to describe privacy issues in this context – both in terms of what the technology can represent and do, and of what people's assumptions would be about the information gathered about them by pervasive systems – is a hard problem.[280] People don't currently know exactly what they want, what the risks and benefits are, and how to react to being (possibly) constantly in view.

In general, the development of privacy in the world of pervasive computing is a research issue rather than a pressing problem. It may be that research into privacy protection continues alongside research into pervasive networks themselves, and development happens 'just in time' – but another more troubling possibility is that lack of privacy protection is storing up problems for ourselves in the future. In that case, we can expect either some people's privacy will be seriously compromised, or that the potential of pervasive systems will never be achieved because people are too nervous to trust them.

CASE STUDY: RFID TAGGING

One of the most controversial pervasive ideas is radio frequency identification (RFID),[281] a low-cost method of tagging objects in order to identify them to a system, so as to keep tabs on their use and/or movement; they are, in effect, clever barcodes. As with many technologies, their benefits have been somewhat hyped, and the growth of their use has not been as stratospheric as was originally expected; even so, worldwide spending on RFID was about $3 billion in 2006, forecast to grow to about $8 billion by 2010.[282]

RFID tags are placed on objects, and can then be used to collect, store and pass on information. Most tags are passive, that is they have no power source, so that it takes an RFID tag reader to give them enough power to transmit the information they are storing. Active tags, in contrast, have their own power and can transmit.

RFID has several potential uses, but the most common applications are in retailing and logistics (especially for sizeable organisations, including retail giants like Wal-Mart, and branches of government such as the US Dept of Defense[283]). Objects can be given tags to give information about their whereabouts, and/or status (e.g. whether the object in question has been bought, or is still 'on the shelf'). Such information is of course invaluable: a retailing firm could know which goods are being bought where, and at what rate; a manufacturing firm could know exactly where particular components or raw materials were when they were demanded; a transportation firm could trace the whereabouts of goods in transit to an individual warehouse, ship or container; all three could guard against theft from stock. On a wider perspective, many desirable social goods could be achieved more easily with RFID technology: recalling faulty or dangerous items; policing against counterfeiting; providing audit trails to guard against corruption; recycling; tracing stolen goods; maintenance of complex systems (such as aeroplanes) in which each component could be given its own tag to store information about its age and possibly even the conditions under which it has been functioning; or ensuring unique and essential identification in particular contexts, such as the handling of evidence in courts of law, specimens in scientific experimentation, or tissue samples in medical testing.

An RFID tag contains a computer chip and an antenna to send information to the reader. They are typically read over a distance of not much more than one metre, and with the current state of the art, accuracy is not brilliant, often under 99%. The speed of the read, the orientation of the object and the proximity of other RFID tags all affect accuracy. The quantity of data stored is not huge – capacity increases costs. Storage can be read-only or read-and-write. The low-cost applications in the retail industry tend to be read-only containing a unique identifier for the object with all the ancillary information stored on a central database, but a cleverer system could also store dynamic information, such as sensor data describing the conditions in which the object was stored, or GPS data describing its whereabouts. Obviously for most users the main factors influencing design are the costs and the benefits. The important cost factors include not only the tags themselves and the tagging process, but also the requirements of the wider system (such as the sophistication of the readers) and the information needs of the user (what data is actually required to be held by the tag itself).

The barcode system has obviously been important for the development of the retail and logistics industries over the last twenty years or so. The major advantage of the barcode is that it is cheap – it can be printed on an object or its packaging almost for free – but it encodes generic information, not specific to the object, and can't be updated. It also requires a relatively large amount of human (and therefore expensive) action during reading (for instance, scanning). RFID improves on barcodes by showing information about each unique object, can provide a dynamic picture rather than just a static one, and allows greater automation of the reading process.

RFID technology has been the object of some suspicion since the concept was developed. Uniquely identifying an object seems to invite the possibility of omniscient tracing, and one method of tracing people is exactly tracing the objects they own or with which they are associated. As US Senator Debra Bowen asked, 'how would you like it if … one day you realized that your underwear was reporting on your whereabouts?'[284] Much of the nervousness stems from a suspicion that the tag would remain active after purchase, so that information would still theoretically be gatherable from the tag even once its value to the manufacturer or retailer was exhausted. Furthermore, although owners or users of objects are in general likely to be aware that RFID tags are attached to them, without access to a reader they would not have any idea what information they are capable of communicating. Syverson et al, noting the range of objects that RFID tags could usefully be attached to, sketch out the amount of information that a hypothetical 'Mr Jones' might be broadcasting in the year 2020: his wig is saying it is a cheap polyester model, his replacement hip is transmitting its medical part model number, a copy of

Das Kapital is shouting from his briefcase, 30 items of lingerie identify themselves from his bag, while the serial numbers of his €1,500 are also being broadcast.[285]

At the conspiracy theory end of the scale, two more worries emerge: tags can be read from a distance without the knowledge of the owner or user; and they could cross-reference information, for example by recording the credit card number used to purchase the object, thereby creating a powerful link between two unique identifiers. As we have seen, it is unlikely that commercial RFID tags would store that much information, and reading technology is not effective over long distances, but part of the argument against early adopters such as Gillette, Wal-Mart and Tesco is that their interest will lead to refinements of the technology. Thanks to such companies, which only wish to improve their supply chains, we will become used to the sight and concept of RFID tagging, and will therefore be more inclined to sleepwalk into a world in which there will be 'chilling effects on consumers' ability to escape the oppressive surveillance of manufacturers, retailers and marketers.'[286] Certainly some of the more enthusiastic adopters, such as Wal-Mart, have something of a public image problem.[287]

The political and ethical issues take on an additional level of complexity when we note that some RFID chips are designed to be implanted into a human body, one example being the VeriChip from the VeriChip Corporation. Such an implant will be able to identify the owner uniquely (although there is presumably no reason why one could not have the chip removed and implanted into someone else – a small operation is required under local anaesthetic). Naturally, the privacy concerns about such implants have been aired very vocally. But in this book, we will not take seriously the additional charge that RFID tagging is the mark of the beast as prophesied in the Book of Revelation, 'And he causeth all, both small and great, rich and poor, free and bond, to receive a mark in their right hand, or in their foreheads.'[288] Yes, well.

As RFID tags become more common, the privacy issues are pressing harder. The relationship between tag and reader is crucial – we need to ensure that information flows from the tags only to readers whose properties are known, and whose owners are either trusted or suitably constrained in their use of information. This, as with so many privacy issues, is a classic question of control; how do we stop information leaking? In particular, a tag that remains operative could possibly leak information for years.

The simplest idea would be to neutralise the tag completely when it is sold and therefore out of the supply chain so that once it is in the purchaser's bag it is dead, or to attach the tag to the packaging, not to the object itself, so it gets destroyed, or at least dissociated from the object, once the object is accepted by the user. This isn't entirely satisfactory, however, as tagging has post-sale uses (for example, it could provide useful information if the item is returned or sold on, particularly for valuable items such as cars or works of art where provenance is an issue). And not all users of RFID tags will be retailers, whose responsibilities for the object cease at the point of sale – public libraries might wish to use a tagging system for their loans, and therefore will want them to be permanently in operation.

One obvious approach is to allow tags to be written over, so the information they contain and send out can be deleted or changed. So, for instance, details of the new owners of the object could replace the old ones on the tag. The details would be stored on a database, and would not be retrievable from the tag itself – someone would require not only the tag, but also the database entries, so the problem of privacy assurance is transferred from the tag itself to the inherently more secure database. The new owner of the object might have a use for the tags too – for example, cataloguing libraries or CD collections, and recovering stolen goods. However, the standardisation that such an approach would require would add to the expense; there would need to be common languages to allow different readers to understand different tags, and methods to prevent malicious overwriting (if thieves could remotely 'transfer' tags into their own names, then much of the value of the personalisation would be lost).[289]

Some tags are password-protected, but that is not a panacea. In the first place, the processing abilities of tags are so small that passwords can't be very complex, and have to be sent in plain text over wireless links, so can fairly easily be intercepted and understood. Secondly, there is an important complexity issue. If there is only a single password for all the tags, then the system is not very secure at all, and once the password is broken an adversary has access to all the information in the system. If there is a separate password for each tag, the reader could not know in advance which password was required, and would have no option but to try them all. If the organisation had many thousands of operative tags and the reader had to perform several reads per second, then this solution would be very inefficient.[290]

There are other alternatives. For instance, the information 'on the tag' could actually be held by a proxy database. The tag reader would only be able to identify the proxy from the tag, so an adversary reading the tag would get some useful information (i.e. what the proxy was), but the proxy (not being constrained as to memory or processing capacity) could also be kitted out with stronger and more practical privacy-enhancing technologies, such as highly secure passwords.[291] There is still argument about the extra resources that would be needed to put proper privacy protection on a tag, with some researchers arguing that the increase need not be uneconomic.[292]

In the very near future, RFID tags are likely to continue to be used as they are almost exclusively used today – in secure supply chains between trusted parties. In which case, the privacy-supporting technology is less of a priority. However, it is also likely that RFID tags will start to be used in other contexts, where trust between the parties cannot be taken for granted, if sufficiently open standards can be agreed upon. But adding in privacy-enhancing technology will add to the price, so we must also expect the price differential in a market situation to allow privacy to be valued and priced into transactions.[293]

9

GET READY, THE PANOPTICON'S HERE

REVIEWING THE SITUATION

Privacy is currently a political hot potato. Digital technologies and a wired world mean that we have lost track of the information people have about us, and we don't know who is seeing what. Almost everyone – when the problem is phrased that way – is nervous about this brave new world; only the occasional visionary, such as David Brin,[294] claims to be relaxed about the info-glut.

In 1787, utilitarian philosopher Jeremy Bentham devised an ideal sort of prison, which he called a *panopticon*. In it, every prisoner would be observable, without knowing whether he was observed, creating the Orwellian-sounding 'sense of an invisible omniscience'. There were many practical purposes which could be addressed by his suggestion.

> No matter how different, or even opposite the purpose: whether it be that of punishing the incorrigible, guarding the insane, reforming the vicious, confining the suspected, employing the idle, maintaining the helpless, curing the sick, instructing the willing in any branch of industry, or training the rising race in the path of education: in a word, whether it be applied to the purposes of perpetual prisons in the room of death, or prisons for confinement before trial, or penitentiary-houses, or

houses of correction, or work-houses, or manufactories, or mad-houses, or hospitals, or schools.

It is obvious that, in all these instances, the more constantly the persons to be inspected are under the eyes of the persons who should inspect them, the more perfectly will the purpose X of the establishment have been attained. Ideal perfection, if that were the object, would require that each person should actually be in that predicament, during every instant of time. This being impossible, the next thing to be wished for is, that, at every instant, seeing reason to believe as much, and not being able to satisfy himself to the contrary, he should conceive himself to be so.[295]

An observable space determined by 'a simple idea in architecture', to use Bentham's phrase – our digital technologies have created exactly that. Do we have a worrying future ahead of us? Well, complacency is certainly not called for. But we should not be heading for the hills just yet.

In the first place, many of these new technologies solve as many problems as they cause. They provide benefits, but there are associated costs. Technologies cut both ways. A fantastic technology like Google allows us to find the tiny bit of useful information in eye-poppingly enormous repositories. Googling for 'kieron o'hara' or 'nigel shadbolt' in each case produces tens of thousands of hits, but the first one in Google's ranked list is the home page of the co-author of this book – all done, searching through millions and millions of webpages, in *under* a tenth of a second. Google is an indispensable research tool in writing a book such as this one. But there is a converse, which is that bad people can find damaging information too. Google is the first port of call for terrorists planning attacks.[296]

Secondly, the flip side is that even some of the most worrying technologies turn out to have positive sides. Many surveillance technologies help with monitoring environmental degradation, tackling traffic congestion or policing. But we should never forget that bureaucracies are information-thirsty, and will never stop consuming. Indeed, they will never even cut down. They will break or bend their own rules, and any prior specification of how information use will be limited, or data not shared, is not worth the paper it is printed on. Function creep is an absolute reality, and advance agreements and understandings have no effect. The only way to tackle function creep is to monitor use constantly, and never to relax vigilance.

Thirdly, the public is far less exercised by the issue of privacy than commentators. Privacy can become a hot button issue when some big event happens, such as a leakage of sensitive information. But in practice, people are prepared to bargain away their privacy for relatively small improvements in convenience or services received. Visitors to the United Kingdom are always surprised at the huge numbers of CCTV cameras dotted about the place, the highest concentration of surveillance cameras in the world,[297] but far from being unnerved the British public are pretty cool about it all. Of course, this insouciance on the part of voters and citizens may well be foolhardy, and could be storing up trouble for the future. Much of the British stiff upper lip is probably down to the British, unlike many other Europeans, not having much of a history of state misuse of information. Our case study of the UK ID card scheme certainly does not refute the suggestion that its likely costs (in terms of money, of inconvenience for the citizen and of the loss of some liberties) will outweigh the benefits (which will almost entirely be in terms of administrative savings). It certainly looks like a technology in search of an application.[298] The difficulty for concerned commentators is to make the point that privacy is important without sounding lurid or paranoid.

We should avoid broad-brush narratives of the destruction of privacy. There are several privacies, and several arguments against them. The struggle for personal space between the individual and the community takes place on a number of fronts, and we should not expect sweeping victories for either side. There will be small advances here, mini-retreats there. In the background, the astonishing progress of technology will keep changing the context. The assumptions of 1990 do not hold now; today's truisms will seem naïve in 2020.

'A CULTURE OF SUSPICION'

Philosopher Onora O'Neill argued in her 2002 Reith Lectures that we were fostering 'a culture of suspicion',[299] where statements announcing a lack of trust (in the authorities, in scientists, in the press, in our fellow citizens) are commonplace. In such a culture, our statements to pollsters are often contrary to our actions, but the suspicions and rhetoric often prompt excessive responses from the authorities to compensate. To claim that O'Neill is primarily worried about government surveillance schemes as a chief *cause* of the culture of suspicion, as some commentators have,[300] is to misrepresent her badly.

Surveillance is associated with spying and crime, but it turns out that most of the pressure to implement surveillance systems comes from two very different avenues. First, there is the

Weberian imperative to efficiency; governments rationalise errors as being due to uncertainty caused by a lack of knowledge. Although it is arguable that uncertainty is actually inherent in a dynamic, complex situation, more knowledge is sought. And second, there is the bottom-up imperative that comes from citizens' behaviour. We demand strong responses to crime and terrorism, but on top of that, we also register little or no complaint when our liberties are decreased as a result of government's (or companies') drives towards efficiency. We sign up for loyalty cards at supermarkets, we use cash less and less, and we do not vote against governments who promote ID card schemes. In a YouGov/*Daily Telegraph* poll of November 2006, one of the more in-depth polls about the 'surveillance society', many surveillance techniques were actively supported by a majority of people in the UK (see table 1), only 11% thought they were often spied upon, and although 44% thought that the government holds far too much or somewhat too much information about people, 41% thought it was about right, or not enough.[301]

If we examine the order of support for surveillance methods in table 1, a rough rationale emerges in the wisdom of the crowd (at least according to the single poll upon which we have drawn). Techniques are more popular when (a) they counter specific and quantifiable risks, (b) they are relatively unobtrusive and do not impinge on the normal actions of daily life, (c) they operate in public milieux where one would not ordinarily expect to indulge in highly private or intimate behaviour, and (d) they capture events or images of particular events or situations, as opposed to creating a permanent and traceable record of identifying features. These are pretty sound principles.

Table 1 Answers to the question 'Please indicate for each of the following whether you approve or disapprove of it', YouGov/*Daily Telegraph* poll, 28-30 November, 2006. (All figures percentages of the UK population).

Measure	Approve	Disapprove	Not sure
CCTV cameras in banks and building societies	97	1	2
CCTV cameras in tube trains and on buses	93	3	4
CCTV cameras outside pubs	86	7	7
CCTV cameras in high streets	85	8	7
Photographing airline passengers	72	17	11
CCTV cameras in taxis	65	21	14
Roadside fingerprinting of alleged suspects	56	27	18
Speed cameras	50	39	11
Fingerprinting airline passengers	45	37	18
Maintaining results of an individual's DNA on the national database even if the individual has not been charged with any crime or else has been acquitted	37	48	15
Using the chips in ID cards to track the movements of every every individual possessing an ID card	16	70	14
Using high-powered microphones to listen in on conversations on the street	7	79	14

Realism

Principles and pragmatism need to be balanced. If our values, however principled, have no means of practical realisation, then they cannot play much of a role in our lives as we actually live them (except, perhaps, to depress us).

So even if we were keen to enshrine the right to privacy, we have to recognise that the passage and transfer of information is extremely easy to accomplish, and hard to police. Privacy is a normative concept – it tells us how we *ought* to behave towards others – but information is *de facto* unstoppable. We rely on conventions that information won't be misused, and can even draft laws to punish misuse, but we still need transparency and accountability. If it is not possible to discover who misused information, we cannot prosecute them. And even if they could be prosecuted, we may not have the power to deliver any kind of meaningful sanctions. If this is the case with online privacy then our rights to privacy in the online world are so much hot air. If we have rights which we cannot enforce, we have no practical advantage whatsoever.

But this should not lead us to unalloyed pessimism. The Web, for instance, may well be the world's most complex piece of technology, but it is still a piece of technology, and it can be engineered. And it can be de-engineered, or regulated. As we have seen, there are many initiatives to boost the accountability and transparency of online users, and many others that try to help people to behave sensibly as custodians of information about themselves. It may be a struggle to protect our rights to privacy, and it will most likely involve some legislation, cooperation of governments, service providers and builders of hardware and software – as well as a responsible attitude from the rest of us. But there is no reason at this stage to renounce all possibility of preserving (some aspects of) privacy, even in our online world. Even if it is not easy to right a wrong, it doesn't follow that it is foolish or wrong to try.

Awareness

The balance between unwarranted and legitimate intrusion is a fine one. The analysis and exploration of relationships between different pieces of information is often in pursuit of laudable aims. The US Treasury Department employs a variety of approaches to detect money laundering and drug trafficking. Its Financial Crimes Enforcement Network (www.fincen.gov) links hundreds of government databases, which the department routinely mines for patterns of activity to detect anomalous or suspicious transactions. The equivalent agency in the United Kingdom at the moment is The Serious and Organised Crimes Agency (SOCA). They acknowledge that the most effective deterrent to much of the high technology crime that is focused on individuals and organisations is what they term *target hardening*. This is making people aware of what they can do to stop unwarranted intrusion, phishing, id theft and a host of other violations.

This education needs to start at a very basic level. Most people are unaware of how the most familiar devices and applications they use compromise their privacy. For example, some software applications routinely associate information about the originating computer with the files they generate. When you mail out a Microsoft Word document you may be inadvertently distributing a whole slew of information about previous versions of the document, edits and changes you have made and so on. And this doesn't begin to address the issues of cookies, Internet browsers, and privacy within our imagined firewalls.

People and organizations are extraordinarily casual with the devices that hold such important and private information. Take the second-hand market for digital devices. Students from the Massachusetts Institute of Technology have described how they analysed a batch of second-hand hard drives. You might have thought that, being obtained from reputable resellers, these drives would have been reasonably erased. However, the students were able to resurrect a wide variety of sensitive information. This included a drive that was formerly part of an ATM machine containing vast quantities of account transaction information. Other discs contained credit card numbers, emails, letters of a sensitive medical nature, and so on. Their study shows that the used hard drive market is awash with confidential information. Software developers surely have the opportunity here to build systems that are smart enough to recognize when to sanitize and completely erase deleted files from our hard drives. A simple utility from drive vendors to rapidly remove all hard drive information would be a start. Why doesn't the industry help us out here?

Technology can be misused, but if you are genuinely concerned about your privacy, one of the most effective things you can do is to take care what you post online. Blogs and photos of drunken or sexy exploits would be much harder to misuse if they weren't posted on MySpace or Photobucket. It is reasonable to assume that anyone interested in you will Google you, in which case you might as well assume that your MySpace page, and your friends' pages for that matter, are stapled to your CV. The World

Wide Web is built to promote the serendipitous reuse of information. Hence one should expect to find stuff copied, linked to or incorporated in other documents. One should not rely on anonymity in McLuhan's global village.

In particular, the law is not going to sort everything out on its own. The Internet is a highly distributed technology, made up of connections between machines in very different jurisdictions. Of course, every machine is in some jurisdiction, but the Internet as a whole is international and cannot easily be brought under one prevailing legal framework. Furthermore, many of the signals one expects to receive in the offline world do not obtain online. One is often alerted to the potential illegality of printed material by the difficulty of getting hold of it; if something is on sale in Wal-Mart that is a signal that it is legal, whereas if one has to enter an anonymous shop up a back street in a sleazy part of town that sends quite another signal. But online these cues do not exist. Awareness involves being much more engaged with the legal and technological situation.[302]

Those using digital information technologies leave all sorts of trails behind them. One does not have to, but to avoid it one would have to eschew mobile phones, credit cards, Internet connections, driving in congestion charge zones or on toll roads, filling in questionnaires and so on. In other words, one would have to live an almost paranoid existence merely in order to return to the level of privacy that one might have expected as recently as 1980.[303] One of the more specious arguments made by the United Kingdom government during the debates leading up to the Identity Cards Act was that their plan that anyone applying for a passport must also apply for an ID card did not constitute compulsion, because no-one was compelled to apply for a passport.

Of course one could not travel abroad, not use a mobile, use cash as much as possible etc. Many green campaigners would like a less hi-tech world, with less consumption and travel, which presumably would be a much more private world. But one's life would be difficult in the twenty-first century, one would miss out on a lot of opportunities and there is very little evidence that many people are enthused by such an austere vision of existence. It is much more likely that we will continue to use the gadgets that roll off the shelves. Some brave souls will risk prison by cutting up their ID cards,[304] but most people will accept it, with a shrug, and will love their government a tiny bit less.

There is a dilemma in a hi-tech age about how far to accommodate small minorities of refuseniks. The more people hold out against a technology, the stronger their position, but as resistance to a technology crumbles (as it usually, but not always, does), it becomes harder for people to make their way in the world without using that technology. The problem often affects older people, poorer people who feel they cannot afford the technology, and sometimes but not always the less educated, and the switch to a new technology will penalise such people disproportionately.

It is virtually impossible to go through life in a Western democracy without leaving an information trail behind, and as this is now the case more good will be done by ensuring that people are aware of that brute fact, rather than by expensively engineering the state's institutions in order to allow some people to opt out. Data protection institutions need to ensure that our brave new world functions safely. As the UK's Assistant Information Commissioner Jonathan Bamford puts it:

I think we have to recognise the fact that if people want to live lives the way they choose to, exploiting modern technology like the internet, like using mobile phones, all those other things which people see as bringing benefit to their lives, there's potentially a danger there that enables their transactions to be tracked, recorded. I think the important thing is that whilst that potential for privacy's been eroded, that actually there is a robust data protection regime which essentially provides that element of space for individuals, so there's not an unwarranted infringement of their privacy. If a mobile phone record is necessary to deal with a very serious crime like a rape or a murder, then that's something which I think as a society we'd accept there's a warranted intrusion into people's private lives. But that isn't the same as that information being fair game more generally for commercial purposes or more generally for government purposes.[305]

So we need to be careful about what we do, and we need to be aware of the protections against harm that we have in law, and their limits. Indeed, a wider, more focused debate on privacy would be welcome; one problem is that filtering and surveillance are arriving in an *ad hoc* way, as new technical methods come on stream, and we are lacking formal evaluations of the policing of cyberspace conducted under democratic conditions.[306]

The commercial situation surrounding privacy and security isn't entirely satisfactory either, thanks to a mismatch between the understanding of the situation by senior management and IT departments. Many managers hope that buying the best technology, maintained by the best techies, will solve the problem. But as we have discovered, people and systems matter at least as much as the hardware and software. Hackers and viruses are bad, but most damage done to privacy is through poor information management by employees, insecure wireless access points, lost and stolen laptops, the failure to retrieve information from ex-employees and so on. Much more important than technology is ensuring that employees have incentives to respect others' information and privacy, and that appropriate policies and procedures are in place. And those policies have to be endorsed by senior managers, not the IT guys; employees have to be aware of the importance that management places on security and privacy. Indeed, a Chief Privacy or Security Officer should be a vital part of senior management at board level; the right message needs to be sent throughout firms and organisations that risks to information are potentially as large and damaging as other risks that are routinely managed or insured against.[307]

As far as our own personal information resources are concerned, we need to be alert to the security risks from attack from without. Owners of PCs connected to the Internet need to ensure that they have installed firewalls and virus checkers, and that security systems are kept up to date. Most operating systems will update automatically with patches when security breaches are discovered.

Keeping up to date is essential. The key moment for security is not the discovery of the flaw in the OS, but rather the moment the patch is publicised. The flaw will have existed for as long as the OS, but is perfectly harmless until someone discovers it. The discoverer, usually, will be an employee or an agent of the developer – developers continue to test their systems rigorously, even after they have been released onto the market. In that case, there is still no danger, as the developer will not wish to undermine its own OS for obvious reasons. The developers can then commission top secret work to create a patch that will seal the breach and remove the security flaw. In this case the *discovery* of the flaw is not a problem.

Once the patch has been developed, the developer needs to get it to all the people running the affected versions of the OS. *This* is the danger point. The publicity that the developer gives the patch needs to be comprehensive so that users are aware of it. But this will alert cohorts of hackers all of whom will try to work out from the patch what flaw it is trying to correct, and many of whom will be able to develop malware to exploit it. So there is a period between the distribution of the patch and the point at which users have installed it, when their machines are vulnerable and there are potentially very many methods of exploiting their vulnerability. The longer one delays installing the patch, the more vulnerable one's system is. This updating process is usually automated, and so happens very quickly. But if one has neglected setting one's security upgrades correctly, one could be in danger of attack. Again, awareness is the key.

We also need to be aware of what is protected and what isn't. For instance, vigilance on the part of the user will be enough to foil (or phoil?) a phishing attack – the information which a bank will ask for online should be strictly limited, and one should not part with any more than that – certainly not a password or PIN number. Close inspection of a phishing email will also often reveal obvious errors in the English, poor spelling, misplaced logos and so on. There are important cues on one's browser, such as the address, the status bar and the security status which many users ignore, leading to incorrect choices being made. In a small-scale experiment, a quarter of the participants did not look at, or understand, the signals of trustworthiness in a website.[308]

Awareness of the technology and strength of online presence between them make an important matrix which shows how online privacy can be unevenly distributed, and makes it an issue of justice and fairness. Market solutions to the problem of online privacy depend on consumers being well enough informed to buy the right privacy-enhancing technologies, setting up the right firewalls and so on, but that information is constantly changing and the effort involved may be more than many people can manage. As society moves more functions online, more people will move from being relatively safe to leading a riskier online life, and this will happen to some people without their knowledge or consent. We may find ourselves divided into privacy-haves and privacy-have-nots.[309] Empirical evidence backs this up. A survey conducted by the Oxford Internet Institute discovered that while people who do not use the Internet at all do not trust it, neophyte users have if anything too much trust. Those without expertise fail to gain experience and are more likely to distrust the technology and not to benefit from it, while new users are very vulnerable. It is experienced users who get the most out of the Internet, trust it more moderately and gain most of the benefits. The distinction between the privacy-haves and the privacy-have-nots maps onto the digital divide, and indeed many of our other social divides.[310]

WHAT TECHNOLOGY CAN DO

The problem is not the technology, except in so far as without the benefits of information technology there would be no costs. Humans are more important than nuts and bolts, chips and wires.

Users of technology need to know what the risks are, what is sensible and what is not. And all technology is part of a social system of administrators, customers, policymakers, managers and security advisors. Not only is every piece of useful technology engineered by humans, but it is surrounded by a support network of humans who manage its use in the real world. Getting the human portion of the system right is extremely important, and easy to neglect. It is the system that means that technology can be used to preserve privacy and serve people, rather than simply being 'technology for technology's sake'.

Privacy preferences are complex and variable across many different contexts. As the online world speeds up and is filled with larger numbers of agents (many artificial), we have an ever-greater need to express such preferences in machine-readable ways. This is doubly problematic – in the first place, people are not used to formulating, and may not be able to formulate, their privacy preferences in a coherent and consistent way, and secondly, it is even harder to do it so that a computer could understand. There are methods beginning to appear that enable people to express their preferences, and that allow companies, organisations and governments to keep track of their obligations. Such methods are perhaps somewhat more mundane than extra-tough firewalls and anti-hacking devices, but many privacy issues arise in the digital world simply because of a failure to communicate preferences, or because an organisation had no way of determining and acting on its obligations. This language-drafting and standard-setting is an essential socio-political activity, and is a key factor in making cyberspace safer.[311]

Personal information is spread widely across the Internet and in databases hither and yon. Information about you is held by a large number of organisations, and it is hard to keep track of. The sum total of all the information that is now out there about an individual – in the open Web or in the structured data bases that exist and can be accessed – is very significant indeed. In England for example we might cite Births, Deaths and Marriages, which have been held electronically from 1982, various forms of the electoral roll, detailed planning applications from millions of individuals, Companies House records holding details on the three to four million company directors in the UK and many others. Together these sources of information are a treasure trove for the Identify Thief. In most countries data protection laws should make it possible for you to find that information and ensure it is accurate. If you had the time and the energy, that is. However, there is no reason why trusted technologies should not be able to scour various sources to bring together automatically, or semi-automatically, the information that is held about you. Such a system would have to be trusted, and very trustworthy, but once the system (by a branded service provider) was in place it should be possible to corral all information relevant to you together in one spot.

One example offering is from Garlik,[312] a company seeking to exploit Semantic Web-style technologies to provide individual consumers with more power over their digital data. As of the beginning of July 2007 it had over 60,000 registered users and was planning to launch its second Data Patrol product. Garlik was set up by the founders of the internet bank Egg (along with Nigel Shadbolt as its Chief Technology Officer). Advisors include privacy experts, lawyers and researchers . The aim of the company is to give people power over their digital identities by showing them what information is out there on the web and in accessible structured databases, how it can be exploited and what steps they might take to reduce the risk of becoming a victim of digital identity fraud.

Garlik attempts to review what is held about people and represent this in a people-centric structure. Data is harvested from the open Web. It also extracts structured and semi-structured data from datasets available free or under licence (for example, the GRO BDM database containing UK births, deaths and marriages, the UK Electoral Roll and many others). This harvesting effort exploits an open source Web crawler and search engine capability. Natural Language Processing is used to find occurrences of people's names, sensitive information, relations to other individuals and organisations.

The company's success to date is based on a strong brand and consumer-facing ethos combined with world class technical infrastructure *and know how*. A key feature of the technological offering is the adoption of Semantic Web capabilities – capabilities which, as we have already discussed, have the power to bring both more precision and much more data linkage to the Web, with all the pros and cons that that implies.

One of the organising ideas behind the Semantic Web is that people should define sets of objects and their relations that they want to refer to or else manipulate in various ways. The areas of defined interest are often described in terms of taxonomies or ontologies describing classes of objects and relations among them. For example, an address may be defined as a type of location, and city codes may be defined to apply only to locations, and so on. Classes, subclasses and relations among entities are a very powerful tool for Web use. We can express a large number of relations among entities by assigning properties to classes and allowing subclasses to inherit such properties.

If city codes must be of type 'city' and cities generally have Web sites, we can discuss the Web site associated with a city code even if no database links a city code directly to a Web site. Once we have this way of linking data rather impressive possibilities emerge. Garlik uses the approach to pull together information about an individual so that the individual gains an appreciation of their vulnerability based on the information that is out there about them.

No review of invasive privacy technologies would be complete without the unification of the information processing power we have reviewed in the last few pages with the sheer might and range of sensor technology on offer. The most striking example of recent years has perhaps been Google Earth[313] which takes high fidelity satellite images of most of the Earth and delivers them via a Web Browser. Property entrepreneurs have used it to identify areas that are ripe to build on and redevelop, and people have seen building extensions that have been erected without planning permission. More encouragingly, humanitarian agencies have used it to measure the amount of damage to villages in Darfur, thus raising international awareness of the scale of the problem. No sooner Google Earth than Google Streets – here high resolution photographs of certain metropolitan areas in the US allow you to travel the streets observing whatever was captured at the time – the young man apparently escaping from a burglary, another man allegedly leaving a strip joint. What price our privacy or anonymity here? As this process becomes more comprehensive and more real-time incidental surveillance becomes a matter of fact.

The quality of optical resolving technology – from phones to cameras, satellites to CCTV is improving all the time, the cost is plummeting, and they are becoming ubiquitous. So it is perhaps irrelevant just how good the resolving power of the best satellite imagery is – probably 5 to 6 inches for Earth orbit – because somewhere and for a substantial amount of the day something has got you in its view; the medium resolution phone picture someone was taking as you walked by, the security video in the shop, the number plate recognition system on the highway and that camera in the sky!

But before we get too alarmed by the technology we should remember that the essential ingredients in the spying game are the individuals, organisations or states that initiate or sanction it. One of the more striking features of the Web-enabling information fabric we now live in is how far individuals can mobilise themselves and others to a common cause. One type of cause is indeed surveillance. There are groups of individuals who through a pervasive communications infrastructure can direct themselves to a particular objective. In Kansas they take photographs of bad driving, post it on the Web, and then have others look out for the offender and remonstrate with them. Another group is dedicated to spotting and tracking celebrities in New York. One member gets a sighting, immediately alerts others and a cyber mob is born. A thousand Stasis can flower. Of course, groups also organise to keep a mutual eye out for people at risk on the land, at sea and in the air. They organise to support the needy, infirm and isolated. Our ability to act in concert is simply being applied to the online world as it has for the last two million years offline. Our technology allows any kind of network to be commissioned, used and decommissioned very quickly.

Tentative conclusions about the brave new world

The key to dealing with privacy online is absolutely not to withdraw from the brave new world; it can be difficult and scary online, but surely the opportunities outweigh the costs. Rather, it is essential that we do not make the facile assumption that the online space has the same properties as the offline space. Instead we need to be aware of the commitments we are making and the risks we are running, and we need to use technology to keep track of what is happening online. The digital world is too large and complex to do everything by hand; it is created by technology, and needs to be policed by technology too.

Moore's Law and the World Wide Web have changed everything. The world is a very different one from the Cold War world. McLuhan's global village has finally arrived, and our business is everyone's business. Changes in technology allied to changes in ideology and a lack of deference to authority mean that transparency has increased dramatically, and we will not be able to return to opacity in the foreseeable future.

If people are aware of the ramifications of what they do, and if they remember that the memory of an action will outlast the moment, and that the audience for a story is much wider than the immediate group of hearers or readers, then they will be able to do what people do so well – negotiate a nuanced set of strategies for disclosing information depending on the context. But they need to be fully aware that the online context is somewhat different from the offline world, in particular with digital 'memories' lasting far out into the future.

We are, in many ways, more transparent to others, but equally the world is now more opaque to the individual. We have argued that we need to be aware of the capability of the technology, the law, and the risks of operating online, but awareness is a problem in another way too. It is very hard to be fully aware of who is doing what to one's personal information. Software tools and Google can help keep track of our online presence, but basically we cannot be certain who is distributing information or misinformation about us, who is using our identities, or what sensors are monitoring us.

Transparency is no panacea for the world's ills, and indeed, if we do not understand the complex contingencies of many people's work and lives, it may actually lower trust.[314] We now act in public, and in return we are able to see others act equally publicly. Secrecy has become much harder, and ever since Watergate it has been a political cliché that an attempt to cover something up almost always has worse results than the original sin. As David Brin points out, most of us would like an asymmetry here – I want *my* privacy, but I want *you* to be accountable.[315] This is inconsistent, and we won't be able to sustain such a model.

But however inconsistent and undesirable these aspects of our brave new world might be, there have been enormous gains in personal freedom, freedom of expression, prosperity and even political power for the individual (as well as extraordinary new vistas in entertainment, work practices and personal communications) as a result of computational developments in the last twenty years or so. The miraculous has become commonplace.

We know that it has changed the powers of the individual immensely. But we also need to be aware that it has changed the nature of the relationship between the individual and the community as well. The privacy which a person could have expected in the 1900s has gone forever, swapped for a plethora of powers, skills and opportunities undreamt of a century ago. We need to ensure we are prepared, equipped and educated for the brave new world, in which we can make so much more of our individuality, while at the same time being part of many more communities, at the global as well as the local level.

ENDNOTES

1. Kieron O'Hara, *Trust: From Socrates to Spin*, Duxford: Icon Books, 2004, 75–92.

2. Samuel D. Warren & Louis D. Brandeis, 'The right to privacy', *Harvard Law Review*, 4 (1890), reprinted in Adam D. Moore (ed.), *Information Ethics: Privacy, Property and Power*, Seattle, University of Washington Press, 2005, 209–225.

3. Kieron O'Hara & David Stevens, *inequality.com: Power, Poverty and the Digital Divide*, Oxford: Oneworld, 2006.

4. '"Intelligent cars" that call emergency services could save lives by 2009', European Parliament press service, 26 Apr, 2006, http://www.europarl.eu.int/news/expert/infopress_page/062–7 652–116–04–17–910–20060421IPR07491–26–04–2006–2006-true/ default_en.htm.

5. IntelliOne, it should be said, has an explicit privacy policy: IntelliOne Technologies Corporation, *Privacy Protection Statement v.2.4*, Dec 2006, http://www.intellione.com/privacy/IntelliOne_ Privacy_Protection_Statement_v2_4.pdf.

6. 'Threads that think', *The Economist Technological Quarterly*, 10 Dec, 2005.

7. 'Demon in the machine', *The Economist*, 3 Dec, 2005.

8. 'What's in a name?' *The Economist*, 5 Mar, 2005.

9. 'What's in a name?'

10. 'The leaky corporation', *The Economist*, 25 Jun, 2005.

11. Charles D. Raab, 'The future of privacy protection', in Robin Mansell & Brian S. Collins (eds.), *Trust and Crime in Information Societies*, Cheltenham: Edward Elgar Publishing, 2005, 282–318, at 285.

12. 'Hey, big-spender', *The Economist*, 3 Dec, 2005.

13. http://www.gearlive.com/index.php/news/article/pot_scented_mp3_player_03280909/.

14. Hugh Muir, 'Wheelie bin microchips could alert councils to big polluters', *The Guardian*, 28 Aug, 2006.

15. Fiona Walsh & Patrick Barkham, 'Animal rights activists tell drug firm's small investors to sell up or else', *The Guardian*, 9 May, 2006.

16. Marc Garcelon, 'The shadow of the Leviathan: public and private in communist and post-communist society', in Jeff Weintraub and Krishan Kumar (eds.), *Public and Private in Thought and Practice: Perspectives on a Grand Dichotomy*, Chicago: University of Chicago Press, 1997, 303–332, and Oleg Kharkhordin, 'Reveal and dissimulate: a genealogy of private life in Soviet Russia', in Weintraub and Kumar, *Public and Private in Thought and Practice*, 333–363.

17. E.g. Carole Pateman, 'Feminist critiques of the public/private dichotomy' in Carole Pateman, *The Disorder of Women: Democracy, Feminism and Political Theory*, Stanford: Stanford University Press, 1989, 118–140.

18. George Orwell, *Nineteen Eighty-Four*, Harmondsworth: Penguin, 1954, 6.

19. Richard A. Posner, 'Orwell versus Huxley: technology, privacy and satire', *Philosophy and Literature*, 24 (2000), 1–33.

20. Ian Black, 'Egyptian blogger jailed for four years for insulting Islam', *The Guardian*, 23 Feb, 2007.

21. Privacy International, *People's Republic of China*, country report, 16 Nov, 2004, http://www.privacyinternational.org/article.shtml?cmd[347]=x-347–83511.

22. Kirstie Ball, David Lyon, David Murakami Wood, Clive Norris & Charles Raab, *A Report on the Surveillance Society*, London: Information Commissioner's Office, Sept 2006, http://www.ico.gov.uk/upload/documents/library/data_protection/practical_application/surveillance_society_full_report_2006.pdf.

23. YouGov/*Daily Telegraph* poll, 28–30 Nov, 2006, http://www.yougov.com/archives/pdf/TEL060101024_4.pdf.

24. Ball et al, *A Report on the Surveillance Society*, 4.

25. Kieron O'Hara & David Stevens, *inequality.com: Power, Poverty and the Digital Divide*, Oxford: Oneworld, 2006, 251–252.

26. Ball et al, *A Report on the Surveillance Society*, 49–63.

27. David Lyon, *Surveillance After September 11*, Cambridge: Polity Press, 2003, 2–3.

28. See in particular John Locke, *Two Treatises of Government*, London, J.M. Dent, 1924.

29. Patricia Meyer Spacks, *Privacy: Concealing the Eighteenth-Century Self*, Chicago: University of Chicago Press, 2003. Jane Austen's *Sense and Sensibility* wittily dramatises the dilemma.

30. Pew Global Attitudes Project, *What the World Thinks in 2002*, Washington DC: The Pew Research Center for the People and the Press, 2002, http://pewglobal.org/reports/pdf/165.pdf.

31. Paul Berman, *Terror and Liberalism*, New York: W.W. Norton & Company, 2003.

32. Kieron O'Hara & David Stevens, 'Democracy, ideology and process re-engineering: realising the benefits of e-government in Singapore', *Workshop on e-Government: Barriers and Opportunities, World Wide Web Conference 2006*, Edinburgh, May 2006, http://eprints.ecs.soton.ac.uk/12474/01/ohara_stevens.PDF.

33. Erving Goffman, *The Presentation of Self in Everyday Life*, Garden City, NY: Doubleday Anchor, 1959, 128.

34. Judith Jarvis Thompson, 'The right to privacy', *Philosophy and Public Affairs*, 4(4), 1975, 295–314.

35. Thomas Scanlon, 'Thompson on privacy', *Philosophy and Public Affairs*, 4(4), 1975, 315–322.

36. Beate Rössler, *The Value of Privacy*, Cambridge: Polity Press, 2005, 43–76.

37. John Stuart Mill, *On Liberty*, especially Chapter IV. In John Stuart

Mill, *On Liberty and Other Essays*, John Gray (ed.), Oxford: Oxford University Press, 1991, 1–128.

38. Rössler, *The Value of Privacy*, 56–66.

39. Cf. e.g. Xiao Qiang, 'The "blog" revolution sweeps across China', *New Scientist*, 24 Nov, 2004, Peter Goff, 'Sex blogger breaks Chinese sound barrier', *Daily Telegraph*, 9 Oct, 2005, Jonathan Zittrain & Benjamin Edelman, *Empirical Analysis of Internet Filtering in China*, 20 Mar, 2003, http://cyber.law.harvard.edu/filtering/china/, The OpenNet Initiative, *Internet Filtering in China 2004–2005: A Country Study*, 14 Apr, 2005, http://www.opennetinitiative.net/studies/china/ONI_China_Country_Study.pdf.

40. 'Inconceivable', *The Economist*, 11 Jan, 2007.

41. Kieron O'Hara & David Stevens, *inequality.com: Power, Politics and the Digital Divide*, Oxford: Oneworld, 2006.

42. Jack M. Balkin, 'Digital speech and democratic culture: a theory of freedom of expression for the information society', in Adam D. Moore (ed.), *Information Ethics: Privacy, Property and Power*, Seattle, University of Washington Press, 2005, 297–354, at 297–301.

43. Samuel D. Warren & Louis D. Brandeis, 'The right to privacy', *Harvard Law Review*, 4 (1890), reprinted in Moore, *Information Ethics*, 209–225, at 210.

44. Warren & Brandeis, 'The right to privacy', 218–219.

45. T. Allen et al, 'Privacy, photography and the press', in Moore, *Information Ethics*, 355–372.

46. Cf. O'Hara & Stevens, *inequality.com*, 243–245.

47. 'Information overlord', *The Economist*, 20 Jan, 2007.

48. Lyon, *Surveillance After September 11*, 57.

49. Charles V. Peña, *Information Awareness Office Makes Us a Nation of Suspects*, Cato Institute, 22 Nov, 2002, http://www.cato.org/research/articles/pena-021122.html.

50. John Wadham, Caoilfhionn Gallagher & Nicole Chrolavicius,

Blackstone's Guide to The Identity Cards Act 2006, Oxford: Oxford University Press, 2006, 11–13.

51. Wadham et al, *Blackstone's Guide to The Identity Cards Act 2006*, 6–7.

52. Wadham et al, *Blackstone's Guide to The Identity Cards Act 2006*, 7–8.

53. YouGov/*Daily Telegraph* poll, 28–30 Nov, 2006, http://www.yougov.com/archives/pdf/TEL060101024_4.pdf.

54. http://www.ips.gov.uk/.

55. Home Affairs Select Committee, *Identity Cards*, report of Session 2003–4, 30 July, 2004, para 197.

56. *Identity Cards Act 2006*, 1.1.2.

57. *Identity Cards Act 2006*, 1.1.3.

58. *Identity Cards Act 2006*, 1.1.4.

59. YouGov/*Daily Telegraph* poll.

60. Wadham et al, *Blackstone's Guide to The Identity Cards Act 2006*, 115–118.

61. Home Office, *Procurement Strategy Market Soundings*, Powerpoint presentation, Oct 2005, http://www.identitycards.gov.uk/downloads/procurement_strategy_market_soundings.pdf.

62. *Procurement Strategy Market Soundings*.

63. 'Mistaken identity', *The Economist*, 30 June, 2005.

64. Charles D. Raab, 'The future of privacy protection', in Robin Mansell & Brian S. Collins (eds.), *Trust and Crime in Information Societies*, Cheltenham: Edward Elgar Publishing, 2005, 282–318, at 300–301.

65. 'Peaks, valleys and vistas', *The Economist*, 18 Jan, 2007.

66. Whitfield Diffie & Martin E. Hellman, 'New directions in cryptography', *IEEE Interactions on Information Theory*, IT-22, Nov 1976, 644–654.

67. Diffie & Hellman, 'New directions in cryptography'.

68. L. Jean Camp, *Trust and Risk in Internet Commerce*, Cambridge, MA: M.I.T. Press, 2000, 85–86.

69. Carl Ellison & Bruce Schneier, 'Ten risks of PKI: what you're

not being told about public key infrastructure', *Computer Security Journal*, 16(1), 2000, 1–7, http://www.schneier.com/paper-pki.pdf.

70. Phil Zimmerman, *The Official PGP User's Guide*, Cambridge, MA: M.I.T. Press, 1995.

71. Camp, *Trust and Risk in Internet Commerce*, 87–88.

72. http://www.sarc-wv.com/.

73. The Interagency Working Group on Cyber Security and Information Assurance, *Federal Plan for Cyber Security and Information Assurance Research and Development*, http://www.nitrd.gov/pubs/csia/csia_federal_plan.pdf, 41–42.

74. Fred Piper, Matthew J.B. Robshaw & Scarlet Schwiderski-Grosche, 'Identities and authentication', in Mansell & Collins, *Trust and Crime in Information Societies*, 91–112, at 92–93.

75. Celeste Biever, 'Beat cybercrime, switch to a virtual wallet', *New Scientist*, 1 Apr, 2006.

76. Piper et al, 'Identities and authentication', 94–101.

77. James Meek, 'Robo cop', *The Guardian*, 13 June, 2002.

78. Piper et al, 'Identities and authentication', 105.

79. Piper et al, 'Identities and authentication', 104.

80. 'Biometrics gets down to business', *The Economist Technological Quarterly*, 2 Dec, 2006.

81. Duncan Graham-Rowe, 'There's no one quite like you', *New Scientist*, 1 Apr, 2006.

82. Piper et al, 'Identities and authentication', 110.

83. Kevin Mitnick, Testimony to US Senate Committee on Governmental Affairs, March 2000, http://www.senate.gov/~gov_affairs/030200_mitnick.htm. See also Kevin D. Mitnick & William L. Simon *The Art of Deception: Controlling the Human Element of Security* (John Wiley, New York, 2002).

84. Information Commissioner's Office, *Husband and Wife Team Convicted of Obtaining Personal Information Unlawfully*, press release, 14 Nov, 2006, http://www.ico.gov.uk/upload/documents/

pressreleases/2006/married_couple_convicted_of_unlawfully_obtaining_personal_information.pdf.

85. Organisation for Economic Co-operation and Development, *OECD Guidelines on the Protection of Privacy and Transborder Flows of Personal Data*, 23 Sept, 1980, http://www.oecd.org/document/18/0,2340,en_2649_34255_1815186_1_1_1_1,00.html.

86. Lorrie Cranor, Marc Langheinrich, Massimo Marchiori, Martin Presler-Marshall & Joseph Reagle, *The Platform for Privacy Preferences 1.0 (P3P 1.0) Specification*, World Wide Web Consortium recommendation, 16 Apr, 2002, http://www.w3.org/TR/P3P/.

87. Electronic Privacy Information Center & Junkbusters, *Pretty Poor Privacy: An Assessment of P3P and Internet Privacy*, June 2000, http://www.epic.org/reports/prettypoorprivacy.html.

88. Helen Nissenbaum, 'Privacy as contextual integrity', *Washington Law Review*, 79(1), 2004, 119–158.

89. Adam Barth, Anupam Datta, John C. Mitchell & Helen Nissenbaum, 'Privacy and contextual integrity: framework and applications', in *Proceedings of the 2006 IEEE Symposium on Security and Privacy (S&P06)*, Washington DC: IEEE Computer Society, 2006, 184–198, http://www.adambarth.org/papers/barth-datta-mitchell-nissenbaum-2006.pdf.

90. Marco Casassa Mont, *Towards Scalable Management of Privacy Obligations in Enterprises*, Hewlett-Packed Trusted Systems Laboratory technical report HPL-2006–45, 16 Mar, 2006.

91. Marco Casassa Mont, Siani Pearson & Pete Bramhall, *Towards Accountable Management of Identity and Privacy: Sticky Policies and Enforceable Trading Services*, Hewlett-Packard Trusted Systems Laboratory technical report HPL-2003–49, 19 Mar, 2003.

92. Marco Casassa Mont, Siani Pearson & Robert Thyne, *A Systemic Approach to Privacy Enforcement and Policy Compliance Checking in Enterprises*, Hewlett-Packed Trusted Systems Laboratory technical report HPL-2006–44, 16 Mar, 2006.

93. *International Perceptions of the UK Research Base in Information and Communications Technologies*, research report, Engineering and Physical Sciences Research Council/British Computer Society, Dec 2006, http://www.bcs.org/upload/pdf/ICT-International-Review-Final-Report.pdf.

94. Gordon E. Moore, 'Cramming more components onto integrated circuits', *Electronics*, 38(8), 19 Apr, 1965, ftp://download.intel.com/museum/Moores_Law/Articles-Press_Releases/Gordon_Moore_1965_Article.pdf.

95. All these milestones taken from Bill Wall, *Computer Chess History*, 23 Apr, 2006, http://www.geocities.com/SiliconValley/Lab/7378/comphis.htm.

96. Electronic Frontier Foundation, *Cracking DES: Secrets of Encryption Research, Wiretap Politics and Chip Design*, Sebastopol, CA: O'Reilly, 1998.

97. Kieron O'Hara, *Plato and the Internet*, Cambridge: Icon Books, 2002.

98. There are many textbooks on data mining. See e.g. Jiawei Han & Micheline Kamber, *Data Mining: Concepts and Techniques*, San Diego: Academic Press, 2001.

99. K.A. Taipale, 'Data mining and domestic security: connecting the dots to make sense of data', *The Columbia Science and Technology Law Review*, 5, 2003, 1–83, http://www.stlr.org/html/volume5/taipale.pdf.

100. 'One grid to rule them all', *The Economist*, 9 Oct, 2004, Tim Berners-Lee, Wendy Hall, James A. Hendler, Kieron O'Hara, Nigel Shadbolt & Daniel J. Weitzner, 'A framework for Web Science', *Foundations and Trends in Web Science*, 1(1), 2006, 1–134, at 46–47.

101. http://setiathome.berkeley.edu/.

102. http://setiathome.berkeley.edu/sah_plans.php.

103. David De Roure, Nicholas R. Jennings & Nigel Shadbolt, 'The semantic grid', *Proceedings of the IEEE*, 93(3), 2005, 669–681.

104. 'Information overlord', *The Economist*, 20 Jan, 2007.

105. For more on NLP, see Berners-Lee et al, 'A framework for Web Science', 50–52, and references therein.

106. Alan Dix, 'The ultimate interface and the sums of life?' *Interface* 50, 2002, 16.

107. Nic Fleming, 'Computers "could store entire life by 2026"', *Daily Telegraph*, 14 Dec, 2006, Ian Taylor, 'Total recall', *BBC Focus*, 174, Mar 2007, 24–27.

108. Kieron O'Hara, Richard Morris, Nigel Shadbolt, Graham J. Hitch, Wendy Hall & Neil Beagrie, 'Memories for life: a review of the science and technology', *Journal of the Royal Society Interface*, 8(3), 2006, 351–365, Gordon Bell & Jim Gemmell, 'A Digital Life', *Scientific American*, March 2007, 40–47.

109. Taipale, 'Data mining and domestic security', 58–60.

110. For reports and estimates on the quantity of information produced annually, see Peter Lyman, Hal R. Varian, Kirsten Swearingen, Peter Charles, Nathan Good, Laheem Lamar Jordan & Joyojeet Pal, *How Much Information? 2003*, School of Information and Management Systems, University of California, Berkeley, 27 Oct, 2003, http://www2.sims.berkeley.edu/research/projects/how-much-info-2003/.

111. Jeremy G. Frey, 'Comb-e-Chem: an e-science research project', in Martyn Ford, David Livingstone, John Dearden & Han Van Waterbeemd (eds.), *Designing Drugs and Crop Protectants: Processes, Problems and Solutions – Proceedings of EuroQSAR 2002*, Oxford: Blackwells, 2003, 395–398, and see http://www.combechem.org/.

112. http://www.ukbiobank.ac.uk/.

113. http://www.stn.org.sg/index.htm.

114. http://www.meb.ki.se/biobank/index.php.

115. http://www.ukbiobank.ac.uk/about/overview.php.

116. http://www.stn.org.sg/03_process.htm.

117. http://www.meb.ki.se/biobank/ethics.php.

118. 'Medicine's new central bankers', *The Economist Technological Quarterly*, 8 Dec, 2005.

119. 'Privacy fears over DNA database', *BBC Online*, 12 Sept, 2002, http://news.bbc.co.uk/1/hi/in_depth/sci_tech/2002/leicester_2002/2252782.stm.

120. Jack M. Balkin, 'Digital speech and democratic culture: a theory of freedom of expression for the information society', in Adam D. Moore (ed.), *Information Ethics: Privacy, Property and Power*, Seattle, University of Washington Press, 2005, 297–354, at 338.

121. On 6 Aug, 1991, http://groups.google.com/group/alt.hyper-text/msg/395f282a67a1916c.

122. Vannevar Bush, 'As we may think', *Atlantic Monthly*, July 1945, http://www.theatlantic.com/doc/194507/bush.

123. Nigel Shadbolt, Tim Brody, Les Carr & Stevan Harnad, 'The open research Web', in N. Jacobs (ed.), *Open Access: Strategic, Technical and Economic Aspects*, http://eprints.ecs.soton.ac.uk/12453/02/Shadbolt-final.pdf.

124. Cf. Lawrence Lessig, *Code and Other Laws of Cyberspace*, New York: Basic Books, 1999.

125. Tim Berners-Lee, Wendy Hall, James A. Hendler, Kieron O'Hara, Nigel Shadbolt & Daniel J. Weitzner, 'A framework for Web Science', *Foundations and Trends in Web Science*, 1(1), 2006, 1–134, at 7–12.

126. Lessig, *Code*.

127. Annik Pardailhé-Galabrun, *The Birth of Intimacy: Privacy and Domestic Life in Early Modern Paris*, trans. Jocelyn Phelps, Cambridge: Polity Press, 1991, 66.

128. Jürgen Habermas, *The Structural Transformation of the Public Sphere*, trans. Thomas Burger, Cambridge: Polity Press, 1989, 51–56.

129. Adam Smith, *An Inquiry Into the Nature and Causes of the Wealth of*

Nations (2 vols), R.H. Campbell, A.S. Skinner & W.B. Todd (eds.), Indianapolis: Liberty Fund, 1976.

130. Adam Smith, *The Theory of Moral Sentiments*, D.D. Raphael & A.L. Macfie (eds.), Indianapolis: Liberty Fund, 1976.

131. Cf. Jeff Weintraub, 'The theory and politics of the public/private distinction', in Jeff Weintraub and Krishan Kumar (eds.), *Public and Private in Thought and Practice: Perspectives on a Grand Dichotomy*, Chicago: University of Chicago Press, 1997, 1–42.

132. E.g. Habermas, *The Structural Transformation of the Public Sphere*, Richard Sennett, *The Fall of Public Man*, New York: Alfred A. Knopf, 1977.

133. Cf. e.g. John Gray, 'The post-communist societies in transition', in John Gray, *Enlightenment's Wake: Politics and Culture at the Close of the Modern Age*, London: Routledge, 1995, 34–63.

134. Though growing, according to some. Cf. Harry Snook, *Crossing the Threshold: 266 Ways the State Can Enter Your Home*, London: Centre for Policy Studies, 2007.

135. Kieron O'Hara & David Stevens, *inequality.com: Power, Poverty and the Digital Divide*, Oxford: Oneworld, 2006, 1–31.

136. Gregg Keizer, 'Phishers pocket $2.8 billion from unsuspecting consumers', *TechWeb News*, 9 Nov, 2006, http://www.techweb.com/showArticle.jhtml;jsessionid=EDBP5MZBPT3XYQSNDLPCK HSCJUNN2JVN?articleID=193700256.

137. Rachna Dhamija, J.D. Tygar & Marti Hearst, 'Why phishing works', *Conference on Human Factors in Computing Systems (CHI 2006)*, Apr 2006, http://people.deas.harvard.edu/~rachna/papers/why_phishing_works.pdf.

138. David Resnick, 'Politics on the Internet: the normalization of Cyberspace', in Chris Toulouse & Timothy W. Luke (eds.), *The Politics of Cyberspace*, New York: Routledge, 1998, 48–68, at 52.

139. Resnick, 'Politics on the Internet', 53–54.

140. Berners-Lee et al, 'A Framework for Web Science', 7–12.

141. Lessig, *Code*.

142. Berners-Lee et al, 'A Framework for Web Science', 107–109.

143. Resnick, 'Politics on the Internet', 68.

144. Samuel D. Warren & Louis D. Brandeis, 'The right to privacy', *Harvard Law Review*, 4 (1890), reprinted in Adam D. Moore (ed.), *Information Ethics: Privacy, Property and Power*, Seattle, University of Washington Press, 2005, 209–225.

145. Balkin, 'Digital speech and democratic culture', 324.

146. Sergey Brin & Lawrence Page, 'The anatomy of a large-scale hypertextual Web search engine', *7th International Conference on the World Wide Web*, 1998, http://infolab.stanford.edu/~backrub/google.html.

147. Berners-Lee et al, 'A Framework for Web Science', 99–109.

148. Tim Berners-Lee, James Hendler & Ora Lassila, 'The Semantic Web', *Scientific American*, May 2001, Grigoris Antoniou & Frank van Harmelen, *A Semantic Web Primer*, Cambridge, MA: M.I.T. Press, 2004, Nigel Shadbolt, Tim Berners-Lee & Wendy Hall, 'The Semantic Web revisited', *IEEE Intelligent Systems*, 21(3), 2006, 96–101, Berners-Lee et al, 'A Framework for Web Science',18–23.

149. Hugh Glaser, Harith Alani, Les Carr, Sam Chapman, Fabio Ciravegna, Alexiei Dingli, Nicholas Gibbins, Stephen Harris, m.c. Schraefel & Nigel Shadbolt, 'CS AKTive Space: building a Semantic Web application', in C. Bussler, J. Davies, D. Fensel & R. Studer (eds.), *The Semantic Web: Research and Applications (First European Web Symposium, ESWS 2004)*, Berlin: Springer-Verlag, 2004, 417–432.

150. Paul Marks, 'Keep out of MySpace', *New Scientist*, 10 June, 2006.

151. Boanerges Aleman-Meza, Meenakshi Nagarajan, Cartic Ramakrishnan, Li Ding, Pranam Kolari, Amit P. Sheth, I. Budak Arpinar, Anupam Joshi & Tim Finin, 'Semantic analytics on social networks: experiences in addressing the problem of conflict of

interest detection', *World Wide Web Conference 2006*, Edinburgh, Scotland, May 2006, http://www2006.org/programme/files/pdf/4068.pdf.

152. Daniel J. Weitzner, Jim Hendler, Tim Berners-Lee & Dan Connolly, 'Creating a policy-aware Web: discretionary, rule-based access for the World Wide Web', in E. Ferrari & B. Thuraisingham (eds.), *Web and Information Security*, Hershey PA: Idea Group Inc, 2005, http://www.w3.org/2004/09/Policy-Aware-Web-acl.pdf.

153. Weitzner et al, 'Creating a policy-aware Web'.

154. Habermas, *The Structural Transformation of the Public Sphere*, 36–37.

155. Hannah Arendt, *The Human Condition*, Chicago: University of Chicago Press, 1958, 55.

156. Arendt, *The Human Condition*, 22–78.

157. 'The enzyme that won', *The Economist*, 11 May, 2006.

158. http://www.technorati.com/.

159. Andreas Kluth, 'Among the audience', *The Economist*, 20 Apr, 2006.

160. http://www.youtube.com/.

161. http://www.flickr.com/.

162. http://del.icio.us/.

163. http://www.myspace.com/.

164. http://en.wikipedia.org/wiki/Main_Page.

165. http://www.mysinglefriend.com/.

166. http://www.illicitencounters.com/.

167. Katie Allen, 'Seeking romance: GSOH and Web 2.0 compatibility essential', *The Guardian*, 12 July, 2007.

168. http://www.tummybutterflies.com/.

169. http://myexperiment.org/.

170. James Surowiecki, *The Wisdom of Crowds: Why the Many Are Smarter Than the Few*, London: Little, Brown, 2004.

171. http://www.aswarmofangels.com/.

172. William J. Baumol, *The Free-Market Innovation Machine: Analyzing the*

Growth Miracle of Capitalism, Princeton: Princeton University Press, 2002.

173. T. Allen et al, 'Privacy, photography and the press', in Moore, *Information Ethics*, 355–372, at 360–361.

174. Jim McClellan, 'Tag team', *The Guardian*, 3 Feb, 2005.

175. Berners-Lee et al, 'A Framework for Web Science', 31–33.

176. Lee Rainie, *28% of Online Americans Have Used the Internet to Tag Content*, Pew Internet & American Life project, 31 Jan, 2007, http://www.pewinternet.org/pdfs/PIP_Tagging.pdf.

177. Fit for Nothing, *08.05 From London St Pancras*, 13 Feb, 2007, http://fit-for-nothing.blogspot.com/2007/02/0805-from-london-st-pancras.html.

178. Jürgen Habermas, *The Structural Transformation of the Public Sphere*, trans. Thomas Burger, Cambridge: Polity Press, 1989.

179. Tim Jonze, 'Death on MySpace', *The Guardian*, 15 May, 2006.

180. Zoe Williams, "'I don't write to titillate. I censor like crazy to make my blogs less erotic'", *The Guardian*, 11 Aug, 2006. Zoe Williams, it should be added, is the interviewer of the blogger, not the blogger herself.

181. http://www.friendster.com/.

182. http://www.classmates.com/.

183. Paul Marks, 'Keep out of MySpace', *New Scientist*, 10 June, 2006.

184. http://imagine-it.org/google/profanegame.htm.

185. http://www.coverpop.com/wheeloflunch/.

186. http://www.virtualvideomap.com/.

187. http://safe2pee.org/beta/.

188. http://www.chicagocrime.org/.

189. Tom Owad, *Data Mining 101: Finding Subversives with Amazon Wishlists*, 4 Jan, 2006, http://www.applefritter.com/bannedbooks.

190. *Roe v Wade*, 410 U.S. 113 (1973).

191. 'Busted flush', *The Economist*, 5 Oct, 2006.

192. 'China imposes online gaming curbs', *BBC Online*, 25 Aug, 2005, http://news.bbc.co.uk/2/hi/technology/4183340.stm.

193. Kieron O'Hara & David Stevens, *inequality.com: Power, Poverty and the Digital Divide*, Oxford: Oneworld Publications, 2006, 167–203, especially 195–203.

194. Cass Sunstein, *Republic.com*, Princeton: Princeton University Press, 2001.

195. Olivier Roy, *Globalized Islam: The Search for a New Ummah*, New York: Columbia University Press.

196. Peter Popham, 'Teenager admits to killing writer, but has "no regrets"', *The Independent*, 22 Jan, 2007.

197. Cf. e.g. Colin A. Ronan & Joseph Needham, *The Shorter Science and Civilisation in China Volume 1*, Cambridge: Cambridge University Press, 1978, especially 78ff.

198. Qiu Xioalong, *Death of a Red Heroine*, London: Sceptre, 2006, 369.

199. Cf. e.g. Bonnie S. McDougall, 'Particulars and universals: studies on Chinese privacy', in Bonnie S. McDougall & Anders Hansson (eds.), *Chinese Concepts of Privacy*, Leiden: Brill, 2002, 3–24, and Maria Khayutina, 'Studying the private sphere of the Ancient Chinese nobility through the inscriptions on bronze ritual vessels', in McDougall & Hansson, *Chinese Concepts of Privacy*, 81–96, at 82–84.

200. E.g. Patricia Ebrey, 'The economic and social history of the Later Han', in Denis Twitchett & Michael Loewe (eds.), *The Cambridge History of China Volume 1: The Ch'in and Han Empires 221B.C.– A.D. 220*, Cambridge: Cambridge University Press, 1986, 608–648, at 641.

201. Ha Jin, *Waiting*, London: William Heinemann, 2000.

202. Gao Xingjian, *One Man's Bible* (Mabel Lee trans.), Sydney: HarperCollins, 2002.

203. For a discussion of the influence of the PAP on Singaporean politics, see Diane K. Mauzy & R.S. Milne, *Singapore Politics Under the People's Action Party*, London: Routledge, 2002. For the key

statement of Singaporean values, see the illuminating memoir by the PAP's founding father, Lee Kuan Yew, *From Third World to First: The Singapore Story 1965–2000: Singapore and the Asian Economic Boom*, New York: HarperCollins, 2000, especially 3–223.

204. Kieron O'Hara & David Stevens, 'Democracy, ideology and process re-engineering: realising the benefits of e-government in Singapore' in *Proceedings of the Workshop on e-Government: Barriers and Opportunities, World Wide Web Conference 2006*, Edinburgh, http://www.w3c.org.hk/www2006/papers/re-eng_sg.pdf.

205. Mauzy & Milne, *Singapore Politics Under the People's Action Party*, Garry Rodan, *Transparency and Authoritarian Rule in Southeast Asia: Singapore and Malaysia*, London: RoutledgeCurzon, 2004.

206. Privacy International, Privacy and Human Rights Survey 2004, Republic of Singapore, http://www.privacyinternational.org/article.shtml?cmd[347]=x-347–83777.

207. Privacy International survey.

208. *The Qur'an*, trans. M.A.S. Abdel Haleem, Oxford: Oxford University Press, 2004, 2.187.

209. Fadwa El Guindi, *Veil: Modesty, Privacy and Resistance*, Oxford: Berg, 1999, 77–82.

210. El Guindi, *Veil*, 81–82 and passim.

211. Leila Ahmed, *Women and Gender in Islam: Historical Roots of a Modern Debate*, New Haven: Yale University Press.

212. As described, for example, in Carla Makhlouf, *Changing Veils: Women and Modernisation in North Yemen*, Austin: University of Texas Press, 31.

213. El Guindi, *Veil*, 161–185.

214. Olivier Roy, *Globalized Islam: The Search for a New Ummah*, New York: Columbia University Press, 141.

215. Tariq Ramadan, *Islam, the West and the Challenges of Modernity*, trans Saïd Amghar, Leicester: The Islamic Foundation, 2001, 53.

216. 'Drip, drip, dripping', *The Economist*, 6 May, 2006.

217. Amitai Etzioni, *The New Golden Rule: Community and Morality in a Democratic Society*, New York: Basic Books, 1996.

218. Warren & Brandeis, 'The right to privacy'.

219. Ferdinand David Schoeman, *Privacy and Social Freedom*, Cambridge: Cambridge University Press, 1992, 37–52.

220. Amitai Etzioni, *The Limits of Privacy*, New York: Basic Books, 1999, 1–15, 183–215.

221. Etzioni, *The Limits of Privacy*, 213.

222. Etzioni, *The Limits of Privacy*, 213.

223. Schoeman, *Privacy and Social Freedom*, 151–191.

224. O'Hara & Stevens, *inequality.com*, 28–31.

225. Jonathan Zittrain, 'Internet points of control', in Sandra Braman (ed.), *The Emergent Global Information Policy Regime*, Basingstoke: Palgrave Macmillan, 2004, 203–227, at 204–214.

226. http://anonymouse.org/.

227. 'Weird but wired', *The Economist*, 3 Feb, 2007.

228. http://www.internetworldstats.com/stats3.htm.

229. OpenNet Initiative, *Internet Filtering in China 2004–2005: A Country Study*, http://www.opennetinitiative.net/studies/china/.

230. Human Rights Watch, *"Race to the Bottom": Corporate Complicity in Chinese Internet Censorship*, Aug 2006, http://www.hrw.org/reports/2006/china0806/index.htm.

231. Jonathan Watts, 'War of the words', *The Guardian*, 20 Feb, 2006.

232. 'Cat and mouse, on the web', *The Economist Technological Quarterly*, 2 Dec, 2006.

233. Privacy International, *Country Report: The People's Republic of China*, 16 Nov, 2004, http://www.privacyinternational.org/article.shtml?cmd[347]=x-347–83511.

234. Amnesty International, *People's Republic of China: State Control of the Internet in China*, 26 Nov, 2002, http://web.amnesty.org/library/Index/engasa170072002?OpenDocument&of=COUNTRIES%5CCHINA.

235. 'The party, the people, and the power of cyber-talk', *The Economist*, 27 Apr, 2006.

236. 'The party, the people, and the power of cyber-talk'.

237. OpenNet Initiative, *Internet Filtering in Saudi Arabia 2004–2005: A Country Study*, http://www.opennetinitiative.net/studies/saudi/.

238. Diane K. Mauzy & R.S. Milne, *Singapore Politics Under the People's Action Party*, London: Routledge, 2002, 140–141.

239. OpenNet Initiative, *Internet Filtering in Singapore 2004–2005: A Country Study*, http://www.opennetinitiative.net/studies/singapore/.

240. Donald Davies, 'The Bombe – a remarkable logic machine', *Cryptologia*, vol.23 no.2, April 1999, 108–138.

241. Michael Smith, *Station X*, London: Channel 4 Books, 1998.

242. Cf. e.g. Gerhard Schmid, *Report on the Existence of a Global System for the Interception of Private and Commercial Communications (ECHELON Interception System)*, report for the European Parliament 2001/2098(INI), 11 July, 2001, http://www.fas.org/irp/program/process/rapport_echelon_en.pdf.

243. Mark Mazzetti & Tim Weiner, 'Files on illegal spying show C.I.A. skeletons from Cold War', *New York Times*, 27 June, 2007.

244. Gabriel Weimann, *Terror on the Internet: The New Arena, the New Challenges*, Washington DC: United States Institute of Peace Press, 2006, 49–145.

245. Weimann, *Terror on the Internet*, 184.

246. Griffin S. Dunham, 'Carnivore, the FBI's e-mail surveillance system: devouring criminals, not privacy', in Moore, *Information Ethics*, 375–397, Mary De Rosa, 'Privacy in the age of terror', *Washington Quarterly* 26(3), 2003, 27–41, David Lyon, *Surveillance After September 11*, Cambridge: Polity Press, 2003.

247. http://tor.eff.org/, and Lasse Øverlier & Paul Syverson, 'Playing server hide and seek', http://www.blackhat.com/presentations/

bh-federal-06/BH-Fed-06-Syverson-Overlier.pdf for some Power-point slides describing the system.

248. 'Cat and mouse, on the web'.

249. Roger Clarke, *Beyond the OECD Guidelines: Privacy Protection for the 21st Century*, http://www.anu.edu.au/people/Roger.Clarke/DV/PP21C.html.

250. David Brin, *The Transparent Society: Will Technology Force Us to Choose Between Privacy and Freedom?* New York, Basic Books, 1999. Our thanks to David Brin for correcting a number of misunderstandings about his work in an earlier draft of this book. The term 'sousveillance' was coined by Steve Mann.

251. Mill, *On Liberty*, 83–103.

252. The *locus classicus* of this paradigm is Mark Weiser, 'The computer for the 21st century', *Scientific American*, Mar 1991, 94–104.

253. R. Payne & B. MacDonald, 'Ambient technology – now you see it, now you don't', in Alan Steventon & Steve Wright (eds.), *Intelligent Spaces: The Application of Pervasive ICT*, London: Springer-Verlag, 2006, 199–217.

254. http://www.apple.com/ipod/nike/.

255. Kenneth Cukier, 'What the mousetrap said', *The Economist*, 28 Apr, 2007.

256. Kenneth Cukier, 'Overcoming hang-ups', *The Economist*, 28 Apr, 2007.

257. Uwe Hansmann, Lothar Merk, Martin S. Nicklous & Thomas Stober, *Pervasive Computing, 2nd Edition*, Berlin: Springer, 2003, 17–22.

258. Payne & MacDonald, 'Ambient technology'.

259. 'A cash call', *The Economist*, 17 Feb, 2007.

260. B. Warneke, M. Last, B. Liebowitz & K.S.J. Pister, 'Smart Dust: communicating with a cubic millimeter computer', *Computer*, 34(1), Jan 2001, 44–51.

261. See for instance K. Martinez, A. Riddoch, J. Hart & R. Ong,

'A sensor network for glaciers', in Steventon & Wright, *Intelligent Spaces*, 125–139.

262. Michael Reilly, 'Where to find the freshest air in town', *New Scientist*, 9 Sept, 2006.

263. Hansmann et al, *Pervasive Computing*, 413–419.

264. 'Sozzled salarymen', *The Economist*, 17 Feb, 2007.

265. Hansmann et al, *Pervasive Computing*, 421–424.

266. Edward Castronova, *Synthetic Worlds: The Business and Culture of Online Games*, Chicago: University of Chicago Press, 2005.

267. http://www.uncleroyallaroundyou.co.uk/intro.php.

268. Stephen Armstrong, 'Strange Bruin', *Sunday Times*, 29 June, 2003.

269. J. Bulman, B. Crabtree, A. Gower, A. Oldroyd & J. Sutton, 'Mixed-reality applications in urban environments', in Steventon & Wright, *Intelligent Spaces*, 109–124, at 119–122.

270. 'The march of technology', *The Economist Technological Quarterly*, 8 June, 2006.

271. Bulman et al, Mixed-reality applications in urban environments', 121–122.

272. Hansmann et al, *Pervasive Computing*, 189–201.

273. Kenneth Cukier, 'The hidden revolution', *The Economist*, 28 Apr, 2007.

274. A Soppera & T. Burbridge, 'Maintaining privacy in pervasive computing – enabling acceptance of sensor-based services', in Steventon & Wright, *Intelligent Spaces*, 157–177, at 158.

275. Martinez et al, 'A sensor network for glaciers'.

276. Soppera & Burbridge, 'Maintaining privacy in pervasive computing', 161.

277. Soppera & Burbridge, 'Maintaining privacy in pervasive computing', 173–174.

278. Marc Langheinrich, 'A privacy awareness system for ubiquitous computing environments', in *Proceedings of the 4th International*

Conference on Ubiquitous Computing, Berlin: Springer-Verlag, 2002, 237–245.

279. Andreas Görlach, Andreas Heinemann & Wesley W. Terpstra, 'Survey on location privacy in pervasive computing', in Philip Robinson, Harald Vogt & Waleed Wagealla (eds.), *Privacy, Security and Trust Within the Context of Pervasive Computing*, Berlin: Springer-Verlag, 2005, 23–34.

280. Timo Heiber & Pedro José Marrón, 'Exploring the relationship between context and privacy', in Robinson et al, *Privacy, Security and Trust Within the Context of Pervasive Computing*, 35–48, Ian Smith, Anthony LaMarca, Sunny Consolvo & Paul Dourish, 'A social approach to privacy in location-enhanced computing', in Robinson et al, *Privacy, Security and Trust Within the Context of Pervasive Computing*, 157–168.

281. The account of RFID in this case is indebted to D. Luckett, 'The supply chain', in Alan Steventon & Steve Wright (eds.), *Intelligent Spaces: The Application of Pervasive ICT*, London: Springer-Verlag, 2006, 55–63.

282. 'Radio silence', *The Economist Technological Quarterly*, 9 Jun, 2007.

283. 'Radio silence'.

284. Alorie Gilbert, 'Privacy advocates call for RFID regulation', *CNET News.com*, 18 Aug, 2003, http://news.com.com/2100–1029_3–5065388.html.

285. Paul Syverson, Ari Jules & Dan Bailey, 'High-power proxies for enhancing RFID privacy and utility', Workshop on Privacy-Enhancing Technologies, Dubrovnik, Croatia, 30 May-1 June, 2005, http://petworkshop.org/2005/workshop/talks/paul-pets-0505.pdf (Powerpoint slides).

286. Katherine Albrecht, 'RFID: tracking everything, everywhere', CASPIAN (Consumers Against Supermarket Privacy Invasion and Numbering) website, http://www.nocards.org/AutoID/overview.shtml.

287. 'Radio silence'.

288. *Revelation* 13:16. See for instance http://www.tldm.org/News4/MarkoftheBeast.htm from These Last Days Ministry Inc.

289. A. Soppera, T. Burbridge & D. Molnar, 'RFID security and privacy – issues, standards and solutions', in Steventon & Wright, *Intelligent Spaces*, 179–198, at 192–193.

290. Soppera et al, 'RFID security and privacy', 190.

291. Syverson et al, 'High-power proxies for enhancing RFID privacy and utility'.

292. Sarah Spiekermann & Oliver Berthold, 'Maintaining privacy in RFID-enabled environments – proposal for a disable-model', in Philip Robinson, Harald Vogt & Waleed Wagealla (eds.), *Privacy, Security and Trust Within the Context of Pervasive Computing*, Berlin: Springer-Verlag, 2005, 137–146.

293. Soppera et al, 'RFID security and privacy', 197.

294. David Brin, *The Transparent Society: Will Technology Force Us to Choose Between Privacy and Freedom?* New York, Basic Books, 1999.

295. Jeremy Bentham, 'Panopticon', in Jeremy Bentham, *The Panopticon Writings*, ed. Miran Bozovic, London: Verso, 1995, 29–95.

296. Gabriel Weimann, *Terror on the Internet: The New Arena, the New Challenges*, Washington DC: United States Institute of Peace Press, 2006,

297. David Lyon, *Surveillance After September 11*, Cambridge: Polity Press, 2003.

298. 'Mistaken identity', *The Economist*, 30 June, 2005.

299. Onora O'Neill, *A Question of Trust: The BBC Reith Lectures 2002*, Cambridge: Cambridge University Press, 2002, and see Kieron O'Hara, *Trust: From Socrates to Spin*, Cambridge: Icon Books, 2004.

300. Lyon, *Surveillance After September 11*, 58–59.

301. YouGov/*Daily Telegraph* poll, 28–30 Nov, 2006, http://www.yougov.com/archives/pdf/TEL060101024_4.pdf.

302. Jonathan Zittrain, 'Internet points of control', in Sandra Braman (ed.), *The Emergent Global Information Policy Regime*, Basingstoke: Palgrave Macmillan, 2004, 203–227, at 224.

303. Kieron O'Hara & David Stevens, *inequality.com: Power, Poverty and the Digital Divide*, Oxford: Oneworld, 2006, 259–260.

304. According to the YouGov/*Daily Telegraph* poll quoted above, 8% of the British public would refuse to have a card if the penalty was a small fine, 3% would risk a large fine, 3% would risk a short prison sentence, and 3% a large prison sentence. 4% claim they would have a card but destroy it. These figures are surely exaggerated; they had better be, because prison overcrowding would be an issue – Britain's prisons, with their 80,000 places, can house about an eighth of one percent of the total population.

305. Transcript of *Analysis*, BBC Radio 4, 5 Aug, 2004.

306. Zittrain, 'Internet points of control', 224.

307. Tom Standage, 'Securing the cloud', *The Economist*, 24 Oct, 2002, and from a different perspective Lyon, *Surveillance After September 11*, 84.

308. Rachna Dhamija, J.D. Tygar & Marti Hearst, 'Why phishing works', *Conference on Human Factors in Computing Systems (CHI 2006)*, Apr 2006, http://people.deas.harvard.edu/~rachna/papers/why_phishing_works.pdf.

309. O'Hara & Stevens, *inequality.com*, 267–271.

310. William H. Dutton & Adrian Shepherd, 'Confidence and risk on the Internet', in Robin Mansell & Brian S. Collins (eds.), *Trust and Crime in Information Societies*, Cheltenham: Edward Elgar Publishing, 2005, 207–244.

311. Cf. Helen Nissenbaum, 'Privacy as contextual integrity', *Washington Law Review*, 79(1), 2004, 119–158, Lorrie Cranor, Marc Langheinrich, Massimo Marchiori, Martin Presler-Marshall & Joseph Reagle, *The Platform for Privacy Preferences 1.0 (P3P 1.0) Specification*, World Wide Web Consortium recommendation, 16

Apr, 2002, http://www.w3.org/TR/P3P/, Marco Casassa Mont, *Towards Scalable Management of Privacy Obligations in Enterprises*, Hewlett-Packed Trusted Systems Laboratory technical report HPL-2006–45, 16 Mar, 2006, Ian Smith, Anthony LaMarca, Sunny Consolvo & Paul Dourish, 'A social approach to privacy in location-enhanced computing', in Philip Robinson, Harald Vogt & Waleed Wagealla (eds.), *Privacy, Security and Trust Within the Context of Pervasive Computing*, Berlin: Springer-Verlag, 2005, 157–168, Daniel J. Weitzner, Jim Hendler, Tim Berners-Lee & Dan Connolly, 'Creating a policy-aware Web: discretionary, rule-based access for the World Wide Web', in E. Ferrari & B. Thuraisingham (eds.), *Web and Information Security*, Hershey PA: Idea Group Inc, 2005, http://www.w3.org/2004/09/Policy-Aware-Web-acl.pdf.

312. https://www.garlik.com/index.php.

313. http://earth.google.com/.

314. Onora O'Neill, *A Question of Trust: The BBC Reith Lectures 2002*, Cambridge: Cambridge University Press, 2002.

315. Brin, *The Transparent Society*.

Index